ONE DAY IN IVAN DENISOVICH

NOTES

including
- *Life and Background of the Author*
- *The GULAG System*
- *Article 58*
- *Brief Plot Synopsis*
- *List of Characters*
- *Preface to the Original Edition*
- *Critical Commentaries*
- *Critical Essays*
- *Questions for Review*
- *Suggested Theme Topics*
- *Selected Bibliography*

by
Franz G. Blaha, Ph.D.
Professor of English
University of Nebraska

INCORPORATED

LINCOLN, NEBRASKA 68501

Editor

Gary Carey, M.A.
University of Colorado

Consulting Editor

James L. Roberts, Ph.D.
Department of English
University of Nebraska

Cliffs Notes, Inc.   Lincoln, Nebraska

CONTENTS

Critical Essays

Questions for Review

Suggested Theme Topics

Selected Bibliography

ONE DAY IN THE LIFE OF IVAN DENISOVICH
Notes

LIFE AND BACKGROUND OF THE AUTHOR

Alexander Isayevich Solzhenitsyn was born in Kislovodsk, a small resort town in the Caucasus mountain range on December 11, 1918, six months after the death of his father in a hunting accident. Shortly afterward, Solzhenitsyn's mother moved to Rostov-on-Don, a city some 600 miles south of Moscow. Life was extremely difficult there; the young mother and son had to live in thatched huts and, at one time, even in a stable.

Solzhenitsyn attended school there, and in 1938, he entered Rostov University as a student of mathematics and physics. He claims that he chose these fields of study only because of the financial security which they would provide him, but that even at this time, literature was the greatest attraction in his life, a fact that was recognized by his teachers. Thus, he enrolled in a correspondence course in literature from the University of Moscow and even tried to get a role on stage as an actor while pursuing his science studies.

Following his marriage in 1940 and his graduation in 1941, he joined the Red Army immediately after Nazi Germany's invasion of Russia and became an artillery officer. He was promoted to captain in the Battle of Leningrad, but was arrested in February of 1945 for veiled but unmistakable criticism of Stalin in some letters to a friend, in which he alluded to the dictator as "Whiskers," the same allusion used in *One Day in the Life of Ivan Denisovich*.

When he was only twenty-seven, Solzhenitsyn was thrown into prison because of "counterrevolutionary activity" and was sentenced to eight years of forced labor and exile by one of Stalin's infamous *troikas*, courts consisting of three military judges. After first serving in a correctional labor camp and then in a prison research institute near Moscow, the author was finally sent to a special camp in the mining region of Kazakhstan, because, as he claims, he would not make moral compromises with the secret police. It was there, in Siberia, that he conceived of the idea of writing *One Day in the Life of Ivan Denisovich;* like the hero of the novel, Solzhenitsyn had to wear his prison number stamped on the areas of the forehead of his cap, as well as on the heart, the knees, and the back of his uniform.

After serving out his complete eight-year sentence, plus one month, and having had a cancer operation, which he miraculously survived, Solzhenitsyn was released but was forced to live in Siberia, where he found a position as a high school mathematics teacher.

In 1957, Solzhenitsyn was permitted to return to European Russia in connection with a decree of the Twentieth Congress of the Russian Communist Party. He settled down in Ryazan, some 100 miles southeast of Moscow, and continued to teach physics and mathematics until the publication of *One Day in the Life of Ivan Denisovich* in the November 1962 issue of the literary magazine *Novy Mir (New World)*. The novel catapulted him to national and international fame.

The reason for the Soviet regime's acquiescence to the publication of *One Day* was Premier Nikita Khrushchev's attempt to expose some of the horrors of Stalin's reign of terror in order to assert himself in the power struggle following the dictator's death. It was during this brief period of the so-called Khrushchev "thaw" that Solzhenitsyn was allowed to publish his works in the Soviet Union.

The end of 1964 marked the end of the de-Stalinization efforts of Khrushchev, and it also signaled the end of Solzhenitsyn's being officially tolerated. The praise for *One Day* and for his other popular short prose piece, "Matryona's Home," soon turned to criticism and to threats. His candidacy for the Lenin Prize, the most prestigious literary award in the USSR, was defeated, and after he had managed to smuggle a manuscript of his novel *The First Circle* out of the country, his private papers were confiscated in 1965 by the secret police. Subsequently, after much controversy and many debates inside the Soviet Union and in the West, Solzhenitsyn was expelled from the Union of Soviet Writers – thus, in practice, withdrawing all publication privileges from him and forcing him to publish his work abroad by smuggling the manuscripts out of the country. *The First Circle, Cancer Ward, August 1914,* and *The Gulag Archipelago* were published in this fashion.

In 1971, Solzhenitsyn was awarded the Nobel Prize for Literature, but he decided not to go to the award ceremony in Stockholm for fear of not being allowed back into the Soviet Union. While the international fame of having won the Nobel Prize probably saved him from being arrested and imprisoned again, his continued refusal to compromise with the political system, and his steady criticism of his own and some fellow dissidents' treatment, finally led to his forcible deportation to West Germany on February 13, 1974.

Since this time, Solzhenitsyn has made his home in the West, changing his permanent domicile frequently. He continues to criticize the Soviet regime, but he is convinced that any change in Russia will come from within, gradually brought about by the triumph of the inherent goodness of the Russian people, rather than by a violent overthrow of the government. The author has been increasingly critical of the West for not taking a stronger political, moral, and military stance against Soviet international aggression. In addition, he is a vociferous opponent of "detente," since he believes that it will weaken the Russian people's resolve to resist and subvert the Communist regime.

THE GULAG SYSTEM

One Day in the Life of Ivan Denisovich takes place in a "special" camp run by the Chief Administration of Corrective Labor Camps and Settlements, better known by the Russian acronym: GULAG. The new rulers of Russia after the violent overthrow of the Czars dealt very harshly with their former, as well as with their new, political adversaries, and, rather than sending their enemies to prison, they began sentencing offenders to "corrective labor" soon after the revolution of 1917. In the following years, concentration camps were built and were combined with corrective labor camps in Siberia, under the administration of the secret police. It is estimated that by 1929, there were already more than 1 million prisoners in these camps, mainly for political reasons.

The establishment of the Five-Year Plans for the economic reconstruction of the Soviet Union created heavy demands for workers to achieve this drive toward changing the Soviet Union from an essentially agricultural society to an industrial society, and it was difficult to find willing and qualified workers for the construction of canals, railroads, highways, and large industrial centers. Thus, from 1929 on, the Soviet rulers began to depend more and more on forced labor. There were hardly any traditional jail terms handed out any longer; instead, criminals and political enemies were sent to labor camps. These sentences, initially for three-year terms, were based mainly on convictions for violations of the infamous Article 58 of the 1926 Criminal Code (see the essay on Article 58).

The first large wave of forced laborers consisted mainly of *kulaks*, disowned farmers who had resisted collectivization, but soon religious believers of all denominations, members of minority groups and nations, socialists, and engineers (who failed to perform their assigned industrial tasks and were classified as industrial saboteurs) followed them to the camps. It is estimated that in 1940, over 13,000,000 (thirteen million) people slaved in these forced labor camps. In 1937, when many Russians had believed that an amnesty would be declared to celebrate the twentieth anniversary of the Revolution, Stalin instead increased the length of the sentences from ten years to fifteen and twenty years, a procedure which was repeated for the thirtieth anniversary of the Revolution, when the twenty-five-year sentences became standard, and ten-year terms were reserved for juveniles.

During World War II, many soldiers believed to be responsible for the initial Red Army defeats were sent to these camps – as were soldiers like Ivan Denisovich, who had allowed himself to be taken prisoner, and men like Solzhenitsyn who had made critical remarks about Stalin or the Communist Party, and many civilians who had lived "in contact with" the enemy during the Nazi occupation. After the war, they were joined by soldiers who had had contact with the Allies, now the enemy. Captain Buynovsky, whose crime was that he had been assigned as a liaison officer to the British Navy and had received a commendation for his services, is one such example in *One Day in the Life of Ivan Denisovich*. In addition, members of former independent countries like Latvia, Lithuania, and the Ukraine, all of whom were now satellite republics of the USSR, as well as other ethnic and national minorities, were interned in these labor camps in large numbers.

Solzhenitsyn describes the history, the methods, and the structure of these forced labor camps in great detail in his long, multi-volume work, *The Gulag Archipelago*. While Article 58 was repealed in 1958 in the course of a complete revision of the Penal Code, Solzhenitsyn maintains that the GULAG still exists and has, with the addition of the sentences to psychiatric clinics, grown even more vicious.

ARTICLE 58

Article 58, which deals with what are described as counterrevolutionary crimes, is included in the part of the Criminal Code which deals with crimes against the state; offenders of this article are not considered "political" offenders, however. (These are dealt with in another section of the Code.) There are fourteen sub-sections, all of them formulated so broadly that practically any action (or even non-action) could be, and was, interpreted as "a crime against the state."

Section 1: deals with any act designed to overthrow, undermine, or weaken the authority of the power of the state. This was applied to workers, even in prison camps, who were too sick or too weak to meet their quotas; it also covers Ivan Denisovich's "crime" of allowing himself to be taken prisoner. It should be noted that this particular section not only included proven acts of "treason," but, by way of another article of the Code, also included "intent to commit treason."

Section 2: covers armed rebellion, especially with the aim of forcibly separating any part or territory from the USSR. This was broadly applied to all members of annexed nations, such as the Ukraine, Lithuania, Estonia, and Latvia.

Section 3: assistance, rendered by any means whatever, to a foreign state at war with the USSR. This made it possible to send to a labor camp virtually any Russian who had lived in occupied territory during World War II.

Section 4: rendering assistance to the international bourgeoisie. This sent thousands of Russians to the camp who had left the country long before the Criminal Code was passed and who were captured by the Red Army or turned over to it by the Allies upon request.

Section 5: inciting a foreign state to intervene in the affairs of the USSR.

Section 6: espionage. This was interpreted so broadly that it included not only proven acts of transmitting information to enemies of the state, but also included "suspicion of espionage," "unproven espionage," and "contacts leading to suspicion of espionage." Any person who knew or had recently talked to a person accused of espionage could be arrested under the provisions of this sub-section.

Section 7: subversion of industry, transportation, trade, monetary exchange or the credit system. Failure to meet agricultural quotas, allowing machines to break down, and allowing weeds to grow too high were also crimes punished under this section.

Section 8: terrorist acts. This included hitting a party member or a policeman and was also broadened by "threat of" or "expression of intent."

Section 9: sabotage – that is, the destruction of state property.

Section 10: This was the most often and most broadly used section of Article 58. It covers "propaganda or agitation containing an appeal to overthrow, undermine, or weaken the Soviet regime, or to commit individual counterrevolutionary crimes, and also the distribution, the preparation, or the conservation of literature of this nature." Such propaganda and agitation included not only the printing and dissemination of subversive material, but also conversations between friends, letters, and private diaries. Solzhenitsyn's letter to his friend about the "Whiskered One" was such "subversion."

Section 11: This section covered and aggravated any of the previous activities when they were found to have been committed not by individuals, but by "organizations." The minimum number for an organization was two people, as evidenced by the exchange of letters between Solzhenitsyn and his friend. Both were sentenced under Section 11.

Section 12: failure to report reliable knowledge of preparations for, or commission of, a counterrevolutionary crime. Denunciation was elevated to a duty to the state.

Section 13: crimes committed in the service of the Czarist regime, particularly as a member of the Czarist secret police.

Section 14: counterrevolutionary sabotage – that is, deliberate nonfulfillment by anyone of duties laid down, or the willfully careless execution of those duties with a view to weakening the authority and functioning of the state. Many prisoners received second and third terms under this provision.

Virtually all the inmates of the "special" camp described in *One Day in the Life of Ivan Denisovich* have been sent there because of a violation of some provision of Article 58. It is obvious that even the most innocent word or action could have been and, when convenient, was found to be a "counterrevolutionary crime," or, as Solzhenitsyn puts it, "Wherever the law is, crime can be found."

BRIEF PLOT SYNOPSIS

One Day in the Life of Ivan Denisovich describes the daily routine—from reveille at 5 A.M. to lights out at 10 P.M.—in a "special" prison camp in Siberia. The protagonist of the novel is Ivan Denisovich Shukhov, a former carpenter, who has been in several of these camps for the past eight years, serving a ten-year term for "treason."

The novel—one could better call it a short novel or a novella—narrates the events of this day without chapter divisions, recording Ivan's progress through the eyes of an omniscient, third-person narrator who sometimes places himself into the protagonist's mind, recording his thoughts and feelings as Ivan himself would express them (see the chapter on "Style and Narrative Perspective").

When the prisoners are awakened by the sound of a hammer clanging against a steel rail, Ivan does not get up immediately, as is his usual practice. Instead, because he feels feverish, he stays in bed, thinking about the possibility of getting on the sick list. A guard pretends to take him to the punishment cells for his tardiness, but he really only wants Ivan to mop the floor of the guardroom.

After performing this task rather superficially, Ivan has a meager breakfast, and then he goes to the camp hospital, where a young poet-medic checks his temperature and then sends him to work. After picking up his bread ration in his barracks and hiding half of it in a hole in his mattress, Ivan joins the rest of the prisoners for the daily roll call and the frisking, which precedes their march to the worksite.

Ivan's "gang" has been assigned to continue building a power plant, and at the heavily guarded construction site, the prisoners try to find a warm place while the gang bosses negotiate the daily work assignment and the work quota which will determine their food rations. Ivan and his work brigade will lay bricks on the second story of the plant after they prepare the tools and the mortar. This is a job that will fill up the hours and the minutes until their noon break.

During lunch, Ivan is able to trick the kitchen staff into giving his gang two extra bowls of mush, one of which he is allowed to keep for himself. He also picks up a piece of steel which he thinks might be useful later on, and he succeeds in buying himself a cigarette.

After the noon break, Ivan becomes so involved in his task as a bricklayer that he loses track of time and eventually he delays the return of the whole prison detachment because of his feverish perfectionism. After the march back to the camp, the prisoners line up for the regulation body search before reentering the camp. Ivan discovers that he is still carrying the piece of steel he found, which, if discovered by the guards, could lead to severe punishment, possibly death. He panics, momentarily, but once again, he is lucky. He manages to smuggle the piece of steel past the guards.

Later, in return for standing in line for one of his wealthier fellow prisoners, one who has received a food package from home, Ivan is given the man's evening meal ration. After dinner, Ivan is able to buy some good tobacco in another barracks, and he is even lucky enough to receive additional food for guarding a gang member's food parcel during the evening check.

After evening inspection is over, Ivan returns to his bunk and discusses God and the efficacy of prayer with Alyosha, a Baptist prisoner with whom he also shares some of his unexpected "wealth." After a second inspection and roll call, Ivan begins to fall asleep, feeling "almost happy" because of all the "good fortune" which has befallen him during this day.

LIST OF CHARACTERS

MAJOR CHARACTERS

Ivan Denisovich Shukhov

Prisoner S-854, who is the protagonist and focal point of the novel. He has been sentenced to ten years of hard labor and has spent the past eight years in a number of prison labor camps. Given above is his full name, which consists of his first name (Ivan), his patronymic (Denisovich = son of Denisov), and his last name (Shukhov). His last name is reserved for use by the bureaucracy, and in the novel, only the prison authorities apply it to the main character. Personal acquaintances would use the first name, plus the patronymic (Ivan Denisovich), as the title of the book suggests, and very good friends might use the first name, or a diminutive of it – that is, Ivan or Vanya.

Tyurin

The boss of Ivan's "gang," or work brigade. A big, tough man who has already spent nineteen years in prison camps and who knows all the rules and all the ruses. He manages to get the best quotas and work assignments for his men. He began to take an interest in Ivan during their days in the camp at Ust-Izhma. Tyurin is not afraid to stand up to Der, the foreman.

Alyosha the Baptist

A mild-mannered prisoner in Ivan's gang who has been sent to the camp for his religious beliefs. He considers his prison term a blessing because it affords him time to pray and to think about his soul. His religiously oriented code of ethics contrasts with Ivan's existential code of behavior.

Captain Buynovsky

Prisoner S-311 has been in the camp only three months and still has much to learn if he is to survive. Sentenced to twenty-five years of hard labor for illegal contacts with the enemy, he is, nevertheless, a faithful Communist and naively believes in Soviet law.

Caesar Markovich

A rich prisoner and a former film director whose packages provide the work gang with a vital means of bribing themselves into better work assignments. He is an intellectual who feels no common bond between himself and his fellow inmates.

Prisoner Y-81

An anonymous prisoner whom Ivan admires because of his dignified, stoic behavior; he serves as a model for the existential behavioral code which Ivan is trying to live by.

Fetyukov

Once a supervisor in an office, he has chosen scrounging (scavenging) as his method for best surviving the work camps. Ivan considers Fetyukov's behavior debasing and counterproductive in the long-term struggle for survival.

Kuzyomin

Ivan's first gang boss in 1943. He took it upon himself to teach Ivan the methods necessary to survive his ten-year sentence by formulating his "Law of the Jungle."

MINOR CHARACTERS

Pavlo

The assistant gang boss who carries out Tyurin's orders in an impartial and impersonal way.

Ivan Kilgas

A Latvian bricklayer in Ivan's gang; a good worker who respects Ivan for his work ethic. He looks healthy and well-fed since he gets two packages a month from home.

Gopchik

A young prisoner from the Ukraine in whom Ivan takes a fatherly interest.

The Two Estonians

Two prisoners strongly bonded by their common fate as members of an annexed nation. They share everything equally and are inseparable.

Senka Klevshin

A deaf member of Ivan's gang who was an inmate in the Nazi concentration camp at Buchenwald; he led an underground movement there and was cruelly tortured. On his return to Russia, he was sentenced to hard labor for "contacts with the enemy" – in other words: treason.

Nikolay Semyonovich Vdovushkin

The young medic in the prison hospital without any background or experience in medicine. He has been chosen for this task by the prison doctor who fancies himself a patron of the arts and wants to give the young poet "a chance to write." Vdovushkin is generally self-centered and has little sympathy for his fellow prisoners.

Stepan Grigoryevich

The new prison doctor who has established bureaucratic methods for determining who is sick and who is healthy. He believes in work as the best medicine for sick prisoners. Only two prisoners per day are allowed to be ill.

Der (Prisoner B-731)

The sadistic foreman at the construction site. He is reputed to have once worked in a high post in Moscow and is now trying to rise to the position of an engineer in the camp. Without any knowledge of bricklaying, he criticizes Ivan's conscientious work.

Lieutenant Volkovoy

The officer in charge of prison discipline. He has only recently stopped lashing prisoners with his whip. His name is derived from the Russian word for "wolf." He forces the prisoners to give up extra articles of clothing before they march to the construction site in sub-freezing weather.

The Thin Tartar

A cruel prison guard.

Big Ivan

An easygoing, compassionate guard.

Clubfoot

A mess-hall orderly; an "invalid" criminal.

Shkuropatenko

Prisoner B-219; a worksite guard.

16

It should be mentioned that, contrary to the conventional treatment in prison fiction or concentration camp fiction, the Camp Commandant is mentioned only briefly. He never makes a personal
appearance.

PREFACE TO THE ORIGINAL EDITION

One Day in the Life of Ivan Denisovich had been completed in
manuscript form in 1958, but Solzhenitsyn did not submit it for publication until 1961, when Nikita Khrushchev's continued policy of "de-
Stalinization" gave the author some hope that the political climate was
right for getting his short work printed. He sent the novel to Alexander
Tvardovsky, the editor-in-chief of the influential literary magazine
Novy Mir, who made the bold decision to bypass the official Soviet
censorship authorities and to submit the work directly to Premier
Khrushchev. This astute politician immediately recognized the potential propaganda value which the novel could provide for his de-
Stalinization policies and had twenty copies of the work sent to the
members of the Politburo of the Communist Party.

Khrushchev later claimed that it was his personal decision—against
some so-called "opposition" in the Politburo—to let *Novy Mir* proceed
with the publication of the novel. Thus, *One Day in the Life of Ivan
Denisovich* was published in the literary journal on November 21,
1962, in an edition of 100,000 copies. It created a literary sensation
and sold out on the first day, as did a second printing a short time later.

In spite of the limited scope and the relative simplicity of the
novel, Khrushchev—through the persona of Tvardovsky—did not want
to leave any reader in doubt about the intention and meaning of the
work, and so the editor of *Novy Mir* added a preface to the first edition,
entitled "Instead of a Foreword," which has been reprinted in almost
all editions of the novel.

Tvardovsky explains that the topic of *One Day in the Life of Ivan
Denisovich* is unusual in Soviet literature because it describes the
"unhealthy phenomena" of Stalin's personality cult (Stalin's name,
however, is never mentioned explicitly)—thus saying, in effect, that
it is now possible to deal with any and all aspects of Soviet reality
"fully, courageously, and truthfully."

Tvardovsky also says that it is the purpose of the novel and of
its mentor, Nikita Khrushchev, to "tell the truth to the Party and the

people" (note the order of importance of the two terms), in order to avoid such things from ever happening again in the future.

Tvardovsky goes on to affirm that the novel is not a "memoir," or a recounting of personal experiences by the author, but a work of art which is based on personal experience, and which, since it is based on "concrete material," conforms to the aesthetic theory of Socialist Realism.

Because the theme of the novel is limited by the realities of time and place – a Siberian labor camp of the 1950s – Tvardovsky insists that the main thrust of the work is not a critique of the Soviet system but that, instead, it is a painting of an exceptionally vivid and truthful picture about the "nature of man." The novel, the editor stresses, does not go out of its way to emphasize the "arbitrary brutality which was the consequence of the breakdown of Soviet legality," but instead, it describes a "very ordinary day" in the life of a prisoner without conveying to the reader a feeling of "utter despair." Thus, Tvardovsky claims, the effect of the novel is cathartic – that is, it "unburdens our mind of things thus far unspoken [and] thereby strengthens and ennobles us."

It may be unfair to call this preface "political hackwork." Evidence indicates that Tvardovsky was sincere – both in his belief in Khrushchev's liberalization policies and in his disgust at Stalin's personality cult. It is clear, however, that he avoids any outright critique of the Soviet system by insisting that *One Day in the Life of Ivan Denisovich* does not level any criticism at the Soviet social and political realities, but rather, it attacks only the excesses of the Stalin regime, a temporary "breakdown of Soviet legality."

This contention was certainly expedient at the time of the publication of the novel, but it does not hold up under close scrutiny. Solzhenitsyn was, and still is, a firm critic of the Soviet system of government, regardless of the regime in power, and he has reaffirmed this conviction countless times since the publication of this novel. In fact, as late as the 1980s, the author commented that the passing of the Stalin era did nothing to do away with the GULAG system. Indeed, it is the author's contention that the prison camp system has been expanded rather than phased out, and that it now envelops more people than ever before.

It is interesting to note that Tvardovsky, at the end of the preface, apologizes to his readers for Solzhenitsyn's use of "certain words and expressions typical of the setting in which the hero lived and worked" – in other words, for Solzhenitsyn's use of some rather vulgar language, which was typical of the language used in such labor camps. Obviously, the editor feared that he might offend some readers. Authoritarian regimes, both left-wing and right-wing, are notorious for their puritanical prudishness, particularly as regards the descriptions of bodily functions and sexual activity. The prolific use of profanity and the vivid descriptions of sexual activity in modern Western art and literature are seen by many Soviet critics as yet another sign of the increasing decadence and the impending decline of the West. It is ironic that Tvardovsky decided to print the offensive words and phrases, whereas many English editions, in fact, edit or omit them entirely.

Tvardovsky's preface is of interest to the Western reader not so much for its critical astuteness, as it is for its revelation of the political difficulties surrounding the publication of the novel. The editor attempts to justify the critical picture of Soviet life by insisting that the novel focuses on a "temporary aberration," thus trying to steer readers into a very limited interpretation of the work.

Political reality, however, has shown that Khrushchev's liberalization and de-Stalinization policies were a temporary aberration and that the publication of *One Day in the Life of Ivan Denisovich* coincided with the end of the "great thaw." Immediately following the publication of the novel, Khrushchev came under pressure from the conservative, pro-Stalin wing of the Communist party and had to make large concessions to this group in order to survive politically; one of these concessions was the withdrawal of his patronage from Alexander Solzhenitsyn and the eventual exile of the author in 1974.

CRITICAL COMMENTARIES

One Day in the Life of Ivan Denisovich is difficult to classify in terms of traditional literary genres. Solzhenitsyn himself has remarked on the disappearance of the traditional boundaries between genres and the lack of interest in "form" within contemporary Russian literature. Commenting on the form of the work, he states that it is a mixture, something between a short story (Russian: *rasskaz*) and a story (Russian: *povest*). A *povest* is defined as "what we frequently call a novel: where there are several story lines and even an almost obligatory temporal expanse." *One Day,* on the other hand, is more of a short story in the sense that it concentrates mainly on one protagonist and on one episode in his life, but the fact that this one day is seen as being typical of a large segment of Ivan's life, as well as being a description of a number of different human fates, also places the work in the genre of the novel.

In keeping with its short story form, there is no formal subdivision into chapters, but we can distinguish twenty-four distinct episodes which make up Ivan's day. *These episodes have been given "titles" in this set of Notes for the sake of easy reference to any of the twenty-four episodes.*

The episodes are arranged thematically around the three main areas of concern for a typical prisoner: food, work, and the eternal battle against the cruel camp authorities. Formally, the episodes – one might properly call many of them vignettes – are arranged in such a way that scenes describing the harsh camp environment which is a threat to Ivan's survival alternate with episodes which depict his overcoming these threats, showing Ivan's small triumphs over the inhumane prison system.

An Unexpected Trip to the Commandant's

The novel begins with a description of Ivan's waking up to the sound of a hammer being banged against a metal rail, the sound muffled by a thick crust of heavy ice on the windows. Usually, Ivan gets up immediately to begin his battle for survival by doing odd jobs which will bring him extra food, but on this particular day, he feels ill and stays in his bunk.

He listens to the noises of the awakening barracks, afraid that the rumors of an impending reassignment of duties for his work gang might be true. He hopes that Tyurin, his gang boss, can bribe the authorities to let them keep their current work project, since reassignment could mean working without shelter on a bare field for at least a month, and without being able to make a fire. A new assignment could also mean grave illness or death to him and his fellow gang members.

As Ivan makes up his mind to go to the infirmary and put himself on the sick list, he is surprised by the arrival of a sadistic guard, nicknamed the Thin Tartar, who announces that Ivan will have to spend three days in "the can," the prison blockhouse, for not getting up immediately. Ivan is relieved. At least he will get hot food, and he won't be forced to go outside to work. Protesting all the while, however, Ivan follows the Thin Tartar to the Commandant's office, sure that his comrades will keep his breakfast for him.

Solzhenitsyn chooses to open his story at reveille in a labor camp in Siberia, describing his protagonist as he is being awakened. This seems to be a logical place to start an account of a typical day in such a camp, but we must remember that several masterpieces of modern literature use the same technique for their opening scene. In Franz Kafka's enigmatic existentialist novel *The Trial,* the protagonist Josef K. awakens to find himself being arrested for having committed a crime which is never explained. In Kafka's story *The Metamorphosis,* Gregor Samsa awakens from uneasy dreams to find himself transformed into a gigantic, odious insect, without ever finding out explicitly for what reason. Other authors place their protagonists into this state between sleep and waking, where the character and the readers have difficulty deciding whether or not the events to follow are a dream or reality.

On one level, *One Day in the Life of Ivan Denisovich* is certainly a story about the nature of man, defined by his inability to make sense of the universe, surrounded and threatened by forces which he is unable to control or even explain. At this level of meaning, the work aligns itself with those of other existential writers who see human beings trapped in a monotonous daily routine very similar to that of Ivan's labor camp (see the essay on *"One Day* as an Existential Commentary").

This impression is reinforced by the use of numbers instead of names – Ivan is called S-854 by the Thin Tartar – a technique used by many modern writers; for example, it is used by Elmer Rice in his play *The Adding Machine,* and by Karel Capek in *R.U.R.* Interestingly, Solzhenitsyn had originally chosen the title *S-854* for the novel.

Ivan's day begins on a negative note in this first episode. He feels ill, which does not happen often; he remembers the work reassignment, which is possible; and he is surprised by the Thin Tartar, who has come on duty instead of Big Ivan, a humane and lenient prison guard (he is associated with Ivan, the protagonist, because of the similarity of their names). Finally, Ivan is sentenced to three days in "the can," but even here, the counterswing of the pendulum begins: Ivan's sentence is "with work as usual," words which are important to Ivan, because not being allowed to work would be real punishment for him. Ivan is not worried about losing his share of the food allotment: the ethics of survival dictate that his comrades will keep his breakfast for him. We should also note that Ivan, while trying against hope to persuade the Thin Tartar to change his mind about the punishment, does not grovel in a demeaning manner but only protests because it is part of the game.

This opening episode establishes some of the ground rules in the camp – a camp which is, in many ways, a paradigm for Soviet Russian society. Improved conditions can be attained only by bribery. Ivan hopes that his gang boss can bribe the chief clerk not to change their work assignment. This means, of course, that some less fortunate gang will be assigned to the job and exposed to its hardships. Ivan does not waste much sympathy on these fellow prisoners. The struggle for survival demands *some* human decency, of course, but *ultimately*, the law of the jungle prevails.

Ivan remembers Kuzyomin, his first gang boss in another camp, reminding some newcomers that the first one to die is always the prisoner who licks out bowls, puts his faith in the infirmary, or turns into an informer.

Mopping the Guardroom Floor

Following the Thin Tartar across the frozen prison compound, Ivan discovers that he is being taken to the Commandant's office. He is led to the guardroom, where he is told that he does not have to serve his three-day sentence, and he is given orders to mop the guardroom floor instead, which makes him forget about his aches and pains immediately. On his way to get a bucket of water from the well, Ivan observes some of the gang bosses trying to read the camp thermometer: if it reads lower than 41 degrees below zero, the prisoners don't have to march to work, but it is commonly assumed that the thermometer does not work properly.

The fear of getting his boots wet reminds Ivan of a pair of new boots which he lost because of a petty bureaucrat's whim to change prison regulations, an event which he describes as the most devastating blow in his eight years in the camps.

Meanwhile, he does a very superficial job of mopping the floor, and the guards treat him with contempt and – worse – as if he were sub-human. When his task is completed, Ivan begins to ache again, and he decides to go to the hospital after joining his work gang for breakfast in the mess barracks.

Note that in this section, when Ivan discovers that the real purpose of his punishment is to clean the guardroom floor, he is relieved; significantly, his body stops aching as soon as he is assigned work, even though his attitude to the mopping of the guardroom floor is not on the same level as his attitude to his bricklaying is, later on in the story.

Much of the moral force of *One Day* is derived from the matter-of-fact way in which Solzhenitsyn describes the inhuman conditions in the camp. There are no adjectives of indignation or protest in his sober statement that the prisoners do not have to work when the temperature sinks below 41 below zero, and the reader should be horrified to hear the narrator describe without commentary that the water in Ivan's bucket was steaming and that he had to hack through a crust of ice to be able to get the bucket into the well.

The guards, addressing Ivan in dehumanizing terms, complain about his careless mopping performance, not realizing that for Ivan "There's work and work. It's like the two ends of a stick. If you're working for human beings, then you do a real job of it, but if you work for dopes, then you just go through the motions." Ivan does not take any pride in his mopping, since he does not, in this instance, work for "human beings"; when he works for his own satisfaction and for the benefit of his whole work gang, as when he later lays bricks, then he will do a "real job." Even so, this work makes him feel better right away, and his aches return only when the mopping is done.

The guards, faceless and nameless lackeys of the system, have one chance to redeem themselves and show some humanity. When they ask Ivan whether he remembers his wife washing the floor, he responds that he has not seen her since 1941 (the novel takes place in January of 1951; ten years have passed), and he says that he does not even remember what she looks like. For any decent human being, this remark might have at least prompted a rough response from the guards about his wife's looks, anything to show a trace of human interest and compassion. But the guards only continue to berate Ivan's work and to belittle him further. Their chance to prove their humaneness has passed.

Breakfast

Ivan joins his gang in the mess hall, remarking on the routine surrounding the daily meals. Fetyukov, the scrounger, is guarding Ivan's breakfast and is clearly disappointed when the latter shows up to claim it. For the next ten minutes, Ivan concentrates only on his food, even though it has gone cold while he has been away. He eats slowly and carefully, since the time spent eating – ten minutes at breakfast, five minutes at lunch, and another five minutes at supper – is the only time which the prisoners have to themselves. When he has finished his poor meal – cottage gruel, boiled fish bones, and mush (made of "Chinese" oatmeal) – he goes to the hospital block.

Note in this episode that as Ivan pushes his way into the mess hall to claim his breakfast, he comments on the fact that it is sometimes necessary to use physical force to push other prisoners out of the way. As we can see in other episodes, Ivan is capable of aggressive or even rude behavior, even though he is basically a gentle and nonviolent man. Yet there are clearly times when physical force is necessary for him to assert himself in his fight for survival. These acts are not committed maliciously or even with premeditation; they are instinctive actions performed either for self-preservation, or else because they are part of the camp ritual.

On his way to a table, Ivan observes a young man crossing himself before eating his meal, and briefly he ponders the loss of religious customs in Soviet Russia. Solzhenitsyn repeatedly calls this suppression of religion in Soviet Russia one of the worst offenses of the Soviet regime and believes that a revival of traditional Russian religiosity and the eventual overthrow of the regime will go hand in hand. It is interesting to see Ivan, himself not a man of traditional Christian faith, comment somewhat sadly on the decline of religion in Russia.

In this episode, the reader becomes acquainted with Ivan Denisovich's personal code of behavior, which is a mixture of sound advice from experienced prisoners, his personal adaptation to the work ethic, and certain guidelines derived from his background as a superstitious Russian peasant. He accepts without comment the camp code that allows fishbones to be spit onto the table, wiped off, and then ground into the floor, but forbids the prisoners to spit the fishbones directly onto the floor. He eats slowly and carefully, even when he is very hungry or when the food is not very good, and he eats the eyes of the fish in his soup, but only when they are still in place, not when they are loosely floating around in the soup. He has also come to the realization that all prisoners, despite their uniform outer appearance, are different individuals, with different roles and talents; he accepts without misgivings the fact that he himself does not count for very much in his work gang, but he is proud of the fact that there are jobs which are even beneath him and which the other members of his gang will not ask him to do.

A Sicklist Attempt Fails

In this novel, Solzhenitsyn rarely gives us lengthy descriptions of a person's character or of his background. Instead, information about the protagonist and his fellow prisoners is given in small installments as the story progresses and as it becomes important for the reader's understanding of the protagonist. Thus, we have found out so far that Ivan has been away from home for ten years, that he has a wife, that he has spent some time in a camp near Ust-Izhma (where he was sick with scurvy), that he has a vitamin deficiency disease, and that he has lost some of his teeth. But we still do not know why he is a prisoner.

In this episode, we are told that Ivan is now in a "special" camp, a prison camp with particularly harsh conditions. This is Solzhenitsyn's phrase for camps which are designed mainly for opponents of the Soviet regime; these men were sentenced under Article 58 of the Soviet penal code (see "The GULAG System").

Ducking behind some barracks to avoid being caught unsupervised, Ivan makes his way to the prison hospital. On the way, he considers buying some tobacco from a Latvian prisoner who has received a package from home, but he decides to try the hospital first. The young medic, Nikolay Semyonovich Vdovushkin, has no medical background at all; he is a student of literature whom Stepan Grigoryevich, the new prison doctor, has taken under his wing.

As Ivan enters, Vdovushkin is copying out a long poem he had promised to show the doctor and from which he does not want to be distracted by Ivan. After explaining that the maximum daily number of prisoners (two) have already been put on the sicklist, he puts a thermometer into Ivan's mouth and continues to write.

Ivan dreams about the luxurious possibility of being "just sick enough," for three weeks, not to have to work. But then he remembers the new prison doctor, whose therapy for any illness is work; clearly, this doctor does not care about the health of the prisoners at all. By the time the young poet-turned-medic tells Ivan that he has a temperature of just under ninety-nine degrees, Ivan is resigned to go to work, commenting that a person who is cold cannot expect any sympathy from a person who is warm.

In this episode, then, we see Ivan on his way to the hospital, considering changing his plan for getting on the sicklist in favor of buying some tobacco from a fellow prisoner. The reader learns that some lucky camp inmates receive packages from home, a fact of prison life which is investigated throughout the novel.

The person from whom Ivan wants to buy the tobacco (and later on, he does) is a Latvian – that is, he comes from one of the small Baltic countries which the Soviet Union annexed after World War II. The camp population is a cross section of the oppressed peoples of contemporary Russia, and most of the ethnic minority groups are represented. In addition to the Latvians, there are also Ukrainians and Estonians, as well as a Moldavian.

The Vdovushkin episode is one of the most interesting episodes in this novel, since Ivan comes in contact here with a creative writer. Young Nikolay was arrested at the university, presumably for reading or writing seditious material. As an idealistic student-poet here in the camp, however, he has forsaken all of his political ideals. He has, to some degree, become a "tool" of the system, in exchange for an untroubled work time. He follows instructions, copies out a long, probably unimaginative poem ("he was writing in neat, straight lines, starting each line right under the one before with a capital letter and leaving a little room at the side") to please his loudmouthed, know-it-all benefactor. He shows no compassion at all, nor any initiative to ease the lot of the prisoners because he fears losing his privileges. He slavishly defends the inhumane rules of the doctor.

Ivan realizes that if one is cold, he should not expect sympathy from one who is warm – that is, from "an ordinary person" who is warm. But, from a poet, a creative humanist, seemingly, one should be able to expect *some* sympathy.

Vdovushkin is Solzhenitsyn's portrait of the contemporary Russian writer who has abdicated his ideals for small conveniences and who now writes long, unimaginative works in prison as a trustee. Solzhenitsyn is particularly harsh with the young poet because he himself has

made it his dangerous task to demonstrate what path contemporary
Soviet writers should take.

Morning Search and Departure

Ivan Denisovich returns to his barracks and waits for the morning
roll call along with the rest of his work gang. Pavlo, the assistant gang
boss, hands him his bread ration, which Ivan immediately realizes
is half an ounce short of the regulation one-pound loaf of bread. He
decides to take half of it with him to the worksite; the other half he
hides in the sawdust of his mattress, then he sews up the hole.

While the prisoners wait to be frisked in the freezing cold yard,
Ivan makes his way to one of the artist-prisoners to have the faded
numbers on his prison uniform repainted. When he returns to his
gang, Ivan notices that one of the fellows in his gang, Caesar Markovich, is smoking a cigarette, and Ivan is reminded of his own lack
of tobacco. Fetyukov, the scrounger, begs Caesar for "one little drag,"
but Ivan does not beg; he stands by silently. Significantly, it is Ivan
who is rewarded; he receives the rest of the cigarette.

Gang 104, Ivan's gang, is about to arrive at "the friskers," just as
Lieutenant Volkovoy, the feared disciplinary officer, orders the guards
to search the prisoners. Camp rules forbid wearing any extra clothing
or carrying anything out of camp; this law exists in order to thwart
prisoners from wearing civilian clothes under their camp uniforms
and carrying food out with them, hoping to escape. Because of this
rule, the inmates have to undo their coats – even in freezing weather.

Captain Buynovsky, a former Navy officer and a newcomer to
the camp, is caught with a non-regulation jersey on and is forced to
take it off. He protests that this procedure violates the Soviet criminal
code, and he accuses the guards of not being true Soviet people, as
well as being "bad" Communists. This brings him a sentence of ten
days in solitary confinement, a punishment which very few prisoners
survive.

After repeated body counts (the guards are personally responsible
for every single prisoner and will be sentenced to take a missing
prisoner's place themselves), the prisoners finally begin their march
to the different worksites, heavily guarded by armed guards and dogs.
As Ivan marches along, he tries to stop himself from thinking about
his aches and his hunger, and he begins to daydream about his wife
and the village which he comes from.

If we look back at the beginning of this episode, we should focus first on Ivan's return to his barracks. Note that when he receives his bread ration, he is immediately aware that half an ounce is missing. Every food ration, we learn, is short. Why? Because the authorities and trustees charged with food distribution always save some for themselves in order to survive a little better. However, Ivan realistically admits to himself that the people who cut up the bread would not last long if they gave every prisoner honest rations. Food, then, is the most important item in the prisoners' battle for survival.

Ivan keeps one hand on his piece of bread, even while he takes his boots off with the other hand. Any edible item left unattended will be stolen immediately – if not by a prisoner, then surely by an orderly or a guard. Ivan accepts this condition as a reality. There are no misgivings; Ivan simply takes the appropriate precautions. Note, however, that he is not afraid that Alyosha the Baptist, who has the bunk next to him, will steal from him. He knows that the man's religious beliefs won't allow him to become a thief. Later in the story, in one of the key episodes of the novel, Ivan and Alyosha will have a serious discussion about religion and the meaning of life.

After it becomes official that Tyurin, Ivan's gang boss, has successfully bribed the officials into letting Gang 104 keep their former work assignment, Ivan has his prison uniform number repainted. The uniform numbers are mentioned over and over; together with the animal terminology which is applied to the prisoners, the numbers serve to emphasize the dehumanizing conditions in the camp. The counting and recounting of the prisoners before they leave the camp is on a literal level – that is, it is standard precautionary procedure. On a symbolic level, however, the counting and recounting signify the existence of the prisoners not as human beings, but as digits.

The cigarette butt episode continues and reinforces the theme of Ivan's code. Ivan wants the cigarette as badly as Fetyukov does, but he does not demean himself, as the latter does. Fetyukov literally drools and begs for the butt. Caesar Markovich, an upper-class intellectual who feels no great allegiance to any of his fellow prisoners, finally gives Ivan the cigarette butt, but he does so because he dislikes Fetyukov more than he likes Ivan. Ivan, however, is pleased to have bested the scrounger. It is a vindication for the code which he learned from his former gang boss, Kuzyomin.

The frisking episode demonstrates the senseless, cruel camp rules.

To make the prisoners take off extra underclothing in the freezing cold is absurd since it diminishes their effectiveness at work.

Captain Buynovsky is a former Navy officer who has only recently been sent to this "special" camp. He is still used to giving commands and has not understood that survival in a prison camp is not possible by insisting on "rules and regulations." His protest that Lieutenant Volkovoy's frisking orders are a violation of the Soviet Criminal Code is sincere but nonsensical in view of the provisions of that same Criminal Code which sent him to this camp in the first place. Volkovoy (his name means "wolf" in Russian) can tolerate an appeal to legality, but he cannot stand being accused of being a "bad" Communist.

The Captain's quixotic protest nets him ten days of solitary confinement, a punishment that he has little chance of surviving. Ivan is better prepared to survive the brutal rigors of the camp. He realizes that vocal or physical protest is self-defeating, and thus, he lets more powerful people, like Tyurin and Pavlo, look out for his rights.

Ivan also realizes that there are moral limits to the struggle for survival. He believes that when one acts in a demeaning way in order to receive favors (whether it's for a cigarette butt or a place on the sicklist, or a reprieve from punishment), it leads to a loss of self-respect and, eventually, to losing the will to live. Ivan's healthy sense of self-preservation, which is not necessarily always based on being considerate and mild-mannered, refuses to adopt demeaning behavior, and, as a result, Ivan has gained a measure of respect from his fellow prisoners. By adhering to his own "code" of behavior, Ivan has kept himself alive for eight years.

Daydreams of Home and of the *Kolkhoz*

Hungry and still feeling ill, Ivan daydreams about a letter that he considers writing to his wife – while all the time marching along, automatically, toward the power plant, his gang's worksite. He is allowed to write two letters yearly, but there is not much he can write about that might interest his wife. The letters that he has received from her have left him puzzled.

According to her letters, his former *kolkhoz,* the collective work farm of the Soviet agricultural system, is in total disarray. Many of the men did not return to the *kolkhoz* after the war, and those who did return only "live" there; they earn their money somewhere else. Most of the young people have left the *kolkhoz* to work in the towns and in the factories. The agricultural work is done almost entirely by women. Carpentry and basket weaving, once the specialities of his village, have been abandoned in favor of painting cheap commercial carpets from stencils. The collective farm is suffering because everybody is earning easier and better money with these carpets. There is a great demand for them, since most Russians cannot afford real carpets. Ivan's wife hopes that he'll return and become a carpet painter.

Ivan does not like these new developments, and he resents his wife's urging him to take up carpet painting after his release from prison. He wants to work with his hands, either making stoves or doing carpentry. But then he remembers, just as his column arrives at the gates of the worksite, that he cannot go home – even after his release from camp. Nobody will hire a man "convicted with loss of civil rights."

At this point, it is obvious that almost all of *One Day in the Life of Ivan Denisovich* will be concerned with life in a prison labor camp. Very little is mentioned about life in Soviet Russia outside of the camps. This particular episode, therefore, is important because, in it, Solzhenitsyn gives detailed attention to one of the prized institutions of the Soviet system – the collective farm, or *kolkhoz*. Here, the author uses Ivan's daydreams during the march to the worksite as a device to show the depressing facts of an institution which has been deserted by the people charged with making it the mainstay of Soviet agricultural production. Most of the older men have not returned to the *kolkhoz* after the war, and the younger men prefer to work in the towns or in factories, and so the collective farm, administered by corrupt and incompetent officials, is left to women and old men.

The pride which the Russian rural population once had in quality craftsmanship has given way to the desire to make easy money with cheap commercial products – in this case, the three kinds of stenciled carpets, for which there is such a heavy demand because the general population cannot afford quality craftsmanship any longer.

Ivan, like Solzhenitsyn, deplores this disappearance of traditional Russian pride in honest quality work and is determined not to follow the modern trend after his release. But then he remembers that he will be, at best, a "free worker" – that is, a former prisoner who, after serving his sentence, is not allowed to return to his former place of residence.

He will have a hard time finding work, due to the "loss of civil rights" which is included in his sentence. Solzhenitsyn mentions "free workers" several times in the story; there are settlements of such workers close to the camp, with only minimally greater comforts than those available to the camp inmates.

This brief episode is the author's only comment on the deteriorating collective farm system. The subject, however, was of deep concern to Solzhenitsyn, who considered the traditions of the rural Russian population vital to any change in the political system. His story "Matryona's Home" (1963) is devoted solely to the topic of rural life and the innate goodness of the Russian people, a goodness which is slowly but surely being undermined by the corrupt Soviet system.

Some Thoughts on Comrades and Bread

Ivan's gang arrives at the worksite and begins to settle into the daily routine. Meanwhile, Ivan ponders about Alyosha's faith, which allows him to survive without extra food rations. He also thinks about the importance of a good gang boss for the survival of the gang members. Tyurin, his assistant Pavlo, and Caesar Markovich, who has a privileged position in the gang because his two packages per month furnish material for bribing the camp officials, go to the office to get the work assignments for the day, while the rest of the gang seeks shelter around a stove in a repair shop. Ivan, still feeling a little ill, begins to nibble the bread ration which he saved from breakfast, thinking about his wasteful eating habits before he was sent to the camp.

While he eats, Ivan observes some of his fellow gang members: the two Estonians who are inseparable and whom he likes, and Senka Klevshin, a deaf prisoner who was sentenced to jail after having survived the concentration camp at Buchenwald.

When Tyurin returns, he hurriedly hands out work orders to the gang members; they will finish a power plant which they worked on in the fall. Ivan and Kilgas, a Latvian, will lay bricks in the afternoon, but they are first ordered to find some material to cover the three big windows in the generator room, where the gang will mix the mortar. Ivan enjoys the prospect of working with Kilgas; they respect each other as skilled workers.

Soon, they manage to retrieve some roofing-felt which Kilgas had hidden illegally, and they plan to use it now to cover the windows.

This pleases the gang boss, and so he assigns them the important tasks of fixing the stove and the cement mixer.

Of significant note in this episode is Ivan's decision: whether or not he should eat his half bread ration. He remembers how thoughtlessly he once filled his stomach with food back in his village, and how wrong he was to do so. Prison life has taught him that food is to be treated thoughtfully and with respect; he is proud of how much work he has done in the last eight years on so little food.

While Ivan eats, he thinks about some of his fellow prisoners. He likes the two Estonians for their camaraderie and for their support of each other; he thinks that he has never met a bad Estonian. Ivan appreciates most of the minority groups whom he meets in the camp, and he makes negative comments only about Russians, referring presumably to the population in the European part of the Soviet Union.

He accuses these people of having abandoned traditional Russian values and having become corrupted by the system. He praises the minority groups for their unwavering support of each other, for their preservation of their folk traditions, and for their good manners, as well as for having retained their religious beliefs. Later in the novel, Ivan will comment on the fact that the two Estonians see where he hides his food, but he feels sure that they will neither steal from him nor reveal his secret hiding place.

Deaf Senka Klevshin illustrates the absurdity of Article 58 of the penal code; he was taken prisoner by the Germans and was thrown in the concentration camp at Buchenwald, where he led a resistance movement. After the war, however, he was sentenced to ten years' hard work for "allowing himself to be taken prisoner" and for "collaborating with the enemy."

After reflecting on Alyosha's religious faith, Ivan thinks about the god-like power of the gang boss. This thought association is not accidental: in Ivan's world, the gang boss replaces Alyosha's God as the omnipotent authority. As Ivan will state in a later conversation with Alyosha, his (Ivan's) world is based on existential principles, in which metaphysical authorities do not operate. In Ivan's world, the gang boss makes all decisions, and these decisions directly affect the all-important food rations. In comparison to this situation, even the Camp Commandant is unimportant, and, significantly, we never even see this supposedly powerful figure. We see only his lackeys.

While the men wait for the work assignments, they discuss the fact that there has not yet been a blizzard this winter which would prevent them from marching to work. It should be noted, though, that a blizzard could hardly be much worse than the sub-zero temperatures and the winds which they have to endure on this particular day; in addition, they have to make up all lost working days by working on Sundays. Significantly, however, any break in the boring routine is welcome.

After another brief look at the unadaptable Buynovsky and at the disgusting Fetyukov, we observe the gang receiving their work orders. Ivan Kilgas (the Latvian) and Ivan Denisovich Shukhov, both named Ivan, are teamed up. Their identical first names are an indication of their parallel backgrounds as skilled, conscientious workers. While neither one of them is important in terms of the bureaucratic hierarchy of the gang — Caesar Markovich's packages carry more weight there — they are respected for their skill and for their practical problem-solving ability. They may not be fortunate enough to be able to provide food to bribe officials, but they assure the well-being of the gang by appropriating material to keep the bitter cold out of the workroom and by assuring the fulfillment of the work quotas by fixing the stove and the cement mixer. In this sense, they are of equal, or greater, worth than Caesar, the rich intellectual, who has been able to bribe himself out of doing hard work altogether.

The GULAG Work Ethic

This short episode contains a discussion of the work ethic in the camps. Clearly, the system is designed to make the prisoners keep each other working hard in order for the whole group to survive. Tyurin has assigned the Captain and Fetyukov to work together carrying sand because that particular job does not need intelligence; here, we should realize that Solzhenitsyn is being satiric: the Captain has been a Navy officer and Fetyukov has been "a big shot" in a government office.

The work makes the men animated, and they even joke about what they will charge for doing such an excellent job. For awhile, Ivan works with Gopchik, a young Ukrainian whom he likes, and time passes very quickly as they prepare for the bricklaying ahead. After one of the very few, directly sarcastic comments about the Soviet government — which has decreed that when the sun is directly over-

head, the time is 1 P.M. – Ivan has to undergo some good-natured rib-
bing about the fact that his ten-year sentence is almost up, which leads
to his reflecting about the reason for his being in this "special" camp.

In this episode, Solzhenitsyn deals with the old question of why
prisoners work so hard – rather than doing sloppy work or even
sabotaging some of the work projects. In this particular scene, we see
that the work quota system has been designed so that food rations
are tied to the fulfillment of the assigned work. Thus, each prisoner
is anxious for all of his gang members to work hard, because he is
the beneficiary of the results and will suffer if, due to a lack of effort
on the part of any single gang member, the work quota is not completed. The work quota, however, only encourages quantity, not
quality of work.

Other, more sophisticated reasons, are given in the course of the
story to explain Ivan's hard work. First of all, only meaningful work –
that is, work which influences the food rations – is done well: the mopping of the guardhouse floor does not fall into this category, and Ivan
does a sloppy job. In addition, it becomes clear that work, any work,
is better than no work at all.

In this episode, we hear no more of Ivan's aches and pains after
he is given a meaningful task; all thoughts of going on the sicklist
are forgotten. Work, as we see later in the story, serves to bolster an
individual's self-esteem, and work well done (Ivan's brick wall) gives
an otherwise unimportant, faceless prisoner an individual identity.
This is also the reason why Ivan actually does his job well, when it
might be enough to make it look as if it had been done well. Fetyukov,
not used to doing manual labor, has to be forced to work and, accordingly, he performs his tasks unwillingly. Small wonder that he is a
scrounger and a bowl licker.

Also in this episode, we discover a special relationship between
Ivan and Gopchik, a young Ukrainian. Gopchik, in many ways, serves
as Ivan's surrogate son (Ivan's only son died young), and Ivan is trying
to pass on some of his knowledge to the young man. He does not
even mind that Gopchik does not share any of the packages he receives from home, but, instead, eats the contents secretly at night.
Just as Tyurin picked out Ivan upon his arrival at the other "special"
camp, Ivan now adopts Gopchik in a fatherly way.

When Ivan looks up at the sky, he notes that it is almost noon,
and this leads to a sarcastic criticism about the Soviet bureaucracy.

Prisoners are not allowed to carry watches; they have to judge the time of day by the position of the sun. But when Ivan deduces that it is noon because the sun is directly overhead, the Captain remarks that the observation is an outdated superstition: the Soviet Government has passed a law that decrees that when the sun is directly overhead, it is 1 P.M. Ivan wonders naively whether the sun now falls under Soviet law, too.

While most days seem to go by quickly with hard work, the end of Ivan's prison sentence does not seem to come any closer. Ivan, who has already served eight years of his term, is teased about having "one foot already out of the camp."

This teasing is done mostly by prisoners sentenced after 1949 (after the "good old days"), when the previous ten-year prison sentences were converted to automatic twenty-five-year terms. Ivan cannot understand how anybody could survive twenty-five years in a "special" camp, but he also does not really believe that he will be released in two years. He remembers many prisoners with original three-year sentences, who had five years added on at the end of their first term. He would not be surprised to have another ten years added to his term. The best he can do is not to think about the end of his sentence and to accept whatever is in store for him. During this good-natured joking about his impending release, Ivan begins to daydream again, this time about the reason for his being in the camp.

Ivan Considers his "Treason"

In February of 1942, Ivan's unit had been surrounded by the German army, without food or ammunition, so Ivan and some of his fellow soldiers had surrendered. A few days later, he and four others escaped from the Germans and made their perilous way back to the Russian lines, with Ivan and one other Russian being the only survivors. On their return, the two were arrested on suspicion of having been sent back by the Germans to spy on their comrades. Thus, Ivan is in the prison camp for "treason." During his interrogation, he confessed. We are told that he confessed because he knew that if he did not, he would be shot on the spot.

A brief discussion of the differences between a "regular" camp and a "special" camp follows. Ivan thinks that life in their "special" camp is easier, because their camp schedule is a regular schedule, whereas in the other camps that he has been in, mainly logging camps, the prisoners have to work until the quotas are filled, regardless of the time of day. The rations are higher in "special" camps, and the numbers which the prisoners have to wear on their uniforms "don't weigh anything," according to the deaf Klevshin.

In this episode, the reader is again confronted with the absurdity of Article 58 of the Penal Code. Ivan has been sentenced to prison camp for treason, his offense having been not only to "allow" himself to be captured by the Germans—but for having had the audacity to escape and rejoin his forces. Thus, Ivan is guilty under both Sections 1 and 3 of Article 58. But, had Ivan remained a German POW and survived, he would have been sentenced for Senka Klevshin's "crime." This is a true Catch-22 situation.

In the rest of the episode, Solzhenitsyn dispels the notion that a "special" camp is much worse than the hundreds of other "regular" camps; in fact, Ivan comments that the only thing that might be considered worse in their camp is the obligation to wear numbers on their uniforms. In return, the food ration is higher, the work schedule more regular, and the numbers are not really a burden. Ivan and his comrades are not singled out for a particularly harsh fate; many hundreds of thousands of their compatriots in "regular" camps suffer the same fate—or worse.

The Midday Meal Caper

The gang suddenly realizes that they have been so preoccupied with their work and talk that they will be late in the food line for the midday meal. Half the day has gone by, and they have not even begun their assigned work. Pavlo, Ivan, and Gopchik secure bowls for the rest of the gang, and Ivan manages to swindle two extra portions of oat mush (a delicacy, compared to the usual magara weed they are served). Although Ivan is responsible for the extra portions, he must wait for Pavlo's decision. (Tyurin never eats with the rest of the gang, a sign of his privileged position.)

Pavlo finally gives Ivan one of his extra portions (every gang boss gets double portions), and he asks Ivan to take one of the extra portions to Caesar Markovich, who has bribed himself into an office job and thinks it beneath him to eat with the rest of the gang. Captain Buynovsky—ten days of solitary confinement ahead of him—is given the other extra portion.

In this episode, the author also gives us an exact account of the food portions served to the prisoners. There are exactly two pounds of groats—crushed oats for each gang, which makes each man's portion miniscule. However, this amount is reduced by cuts for the cook, for the mess hall orderlies, and for the "sanitary" inspector, a double portion for the gang boss, and extra cuts for the bowl washers and for the friends of the cook. And the groats are considered a delicacy; frequently, they are replaced by magara, a Chinese grass substitute. The author does not bother to state what the actual size of a prisoner's portion is after these reductions.

Once again, this episode concentrates on the daily fight for food and on the power which the gang boss has over his crew. Ivan, who has managed to cheat the cook out of two extra portions, does not even think about keeping one for himself. Instead, he hands both to Pavlo, who makes him wait for his reward until he has finished his regular portion. In the meantime, Solzhenitsyn shows us the Captain, who has been in the camp for only a short time, slowly changing—from being a loudmouthed naval officer, used to commanding—into a cagey and cunning camp inmate. The change, however, is probably too late, in view of his impending punishment. In spite of all the impersonal ritual he has to perform, Pavlo, the assistant gang boss, shows that there is still a trace of humanity left in him when he assigns the other portion of the groats to Captain Buynovsky.

A Discussion of Art

Ivan enters the office to bring Caesar Markovich his bowl of now-cold mush and finds Caesar engaged in a conversation with prisoner K-123, an old man who has already served twenty years. The two are hotly debating the artistic merits of Sergei Eisenstein's famous film *Ivan the Terrible*. Caesar defends the film as a work of genius while the other man condemns it for its vindication of a one-man tyranny, something that would have pleased Stalin very much. When Caesar objects that Eisenstein had to make compromises to get his work past the censors, K-123 violently objects to Caesar's calling Eisenstein a genius: "a genius does not adapt his treatment to the taste of tyrants."

In this very brief scene, Solzhenitsyn gives his critique of a masterpiece of Russian art, Eisenstein's film *Ivan the Terrible*. At the same time, he deals with all his fellow artists who have been willing to compromise with the Stalin regime. In this sense, the episode is a continuation and an intensification of the theme begun in the episode focusing on the young poet Nikolay Vdovushkin (Episode 4). Here, however, Caesar Markovich is an artist and an intellectual; he despises manual labor and has made art his quasi-religion in the camp. Accordingly, the discussion between him and K-123 takes on the sense of being a religious debate (remember, the two contestants are sitting in a comfortably warm office); the debate proves much too sophisticated for Ivan, the naive witness to the conversation. Caesar is not interested in any "political message" that might be in the film; instead, he admires the artistic concept and its masterful execution, and thereby, he insinuates that an artist has no political responsibility. This enrages K-123, who criticizes the film for its vile political praise of a one-man dictatorship. He denies the title of genius to any artist who "adapts his treatment to the taste of tyrants."

K-123 is clearly a mouthpiece for Solzhenitsyn, who, in many letters and speeches to the Soviet Writers' Union, insisted on the personal and political morality of the artist and expressed his open contempt for all of those Russian writers who compromised or collaborated with the Stalin regime in order to get their works past the censors. As will also happen in a later episode, Ivan Denisovich is an uncomprehending bystander here, one who simply waits around to see whether or not Caesar will give him a little tobacco or some of the mush; in many ways, Ivan's simple, traditional, naive values are far superior to those of Caesar, whom both Ivan and Solzhenitsyn view with distrust.

Tyurin's Story

Returning to his workplace, Ivan picks up a small piece of steel, for which he may have some use later, and he puts it into his pocket. Tyurin has managed to get them better work rates, which means more bread for the next five days. Before the signal to return to work after their meal break, the men huddle around the two stoves, listening to Tyurin tell a story.

In 1930, Tyurin was dishonorably discharged from the army for being the son of a *kulak*, a member of the land-owning middle-class who had fallen into disfavor with the Soviet regime for resisting the collectivization of their farms. Ivan borrows a cigarette from Eino, one of the Estonians, and listens to the continuation of his gang boss' story.

After his dismissal from the army, Tyurin says, he managed to get on a train which would take him home. Since train tickets were available only by voucher, he secretly boarded a train and got to his hometown with the help of some girls who hid him under their coats. He later met one of them again, in a labor camp, and he was able to return the favor which she had done for him. Then, when he got home, he took his young brother with him to the south of Russia and put him into the care of a group of street thugs, who would teach the child how to survive. He never saw his brother again. He himself ended up in prison soon afterward, during a wave of arrests directed at the *kulaks*.

This episode could rightly be entitled "Tyurin's Story." It serves to direct interest away from the protagonist for a short time and to demonstrate how many Russians of all backgrounds have been sent to the camps during the Stalin regime. Tyurin's only crime is that he is the son of a *kulak,* a farmer who had understandably resisted the government takeover of his private farm. Rather than expose his young brother to the inevitable wrath of the Stalin regime, he gives him into the care of a street gang, where he might learn the necessary techniques for survival. The power of Tyurin's story, like much of *One Day in the Life of Ivan Denisovich*, lies in the matter-of-fact way in which it is told – with no attributes of anger or sorrow accompanying Tyurin's account of his own fate and that of his brother. Indignation is really impossible because Tyurin's story is not extraordinary at all. It has been experienced by all of his listeners in the camp and by uncounted Russians outside.

There is also a brief glimpse of Ivan's basic, uncalculated humanity when he gives the butt of his cigarette to the deaf Senka Klevshin, whom he pities for not being able to follow the boss' story; before that, he even considers – momentarily – giving the butt to the scavenger Fetyukov, because he feels sorry for him.

The Art of Bricklaying

After his story is finished, Tyurin orders his men to work, although the official signal has not yet been given. Ivan, Kilgas, and Klevshin begin to lay bricks on the second story of the unfinished power plant. Once he begins to work, Ivan does not focus on anything except the task in front of him. For these short hours, he is his own "boss," proud of his skills and eager to win the friendly competition he has with the people who are supplying him with bricks.

Ivan proves to be a master bricklayer, building his wall perfectly straight. Meanwhile, Fetyukov begins to wilt under the strain of work, while the Captain gets better and better, a fact which Ivan acknowledges with small, jocular compliments. Alyosha the Baptist also turns out to be a good worker, good-naturedly following the commands of the Captain. This period of concentrated and united work is interrupted by Der, the construction foreman.

The emphasis in this episode is primarily on work. On Tyurin's orders, the gang immediately begins their daily work – although no official command has been given. Once again, this demonstrates the power of the gang boss who, in Ivan's words, "fed you [and who] wouldn't make you work if you didn't have to." Most of the prisoners to whom the author attributes positive qualities (Ivan, Kilgas, Tyurin, Klevshin, and Alyosha) symbolically work on the upper level of the building, while Fetyukov and the others labor below.

Ivan really becomes immersed in his work. Work is his equivalent to Alyosha's religion and Caesar's art, and he is equally fanatic about it. Indeed, the whole description of Ivan at work can be compared to the description of a religious ritual, of a priest performing a sacred task, aided by some minor attendants. The whole gang seems reduced to providing Ivan with material for his work at the right time.

In stark contrast to Ivan's quasi-religious work ethic is the stance of the foreman who has come to check on the defective electrical hoist. He stands by and watches one of his underlings tinker with the motor. And in contrast also, Ivan thinks only of how much more efficiently he could perform his work if the hoist were repaired.

Foreman Der Is Put to Shame

Der, the construction foreman, who wants to be promoted to engineer, is enraged about the theft of the roofing-felt which Ivan and Kilgas used earlier in the day to cover the windows of the generator room so that the gang and the mortar would be protected from the freezing wind. He threatens Tyurin with an additional sentence for condoning the theft, but the gang boss is not afraid. He warns Der that he will lose his life if he utters a word about the roofing-felt. The rest of the gang, including Ivan Denisovich, is ready to use physical violence to protect their boss. Der becomes afraid and backs down, and as he leaves, Tyurin berates him about the non-functioning hoist and demands that the gang be given better work rates for having to carry the mortar and the bricks to the second story by hand. As the foreman leaves, he weakly criticizes Ivan's bricklaying, but he is cleverly repudiated by Ivan, continuing to shout for more mortar.

Der, the focus of this episode, is a prisoner himself; he was once, however, an official in a government ministry, and he considers himself superior to the rest of the prisoners, even the gang bosses. He has no practical knowledge of the work which he is supervising, and so he tries to improve his position by tyrannizing the inmates. Ivan comments that one should be able to build a house with one's own hands before one hopes to be called an engineer.

Again, Solzhenitsyn contrasts the educated but impractical bureaucrat with the uneducated but handy workman, and he clearly takes the side of the simple man. The former bureaucrat proves as useless as his successors in the Soviet government bureaucracy. The burden of keeping the country going is on the shoulders of peasants, tradesmen, and craftsmen like Ivan, who contemplates that he is, by trade, a carpenter, and yet he can (and easily does) learn a dozen more practical trades, if necessary. In *One Day in the Life of Ivan Denisovich* and in many of his subsequent works, Solzhenitsyn shows his deep distrust of intellectuals and bureaucrats; he indicates that any hope for a regeneration of Russia will have to be found within the common, rural Russian population.

Ivan's Zealous Perfectionism

Reflecting on the run-in with Der, Ivan concludes that machines cannot be trusted, because they always tend to break down. Meanwhile, the work is proceeding fast, and there is more mortar left than the gang can reasonably use before their return to camp. The other gangs at the worksite have already handed in their tools and are getting ready for their return, but Ivan is unwilling to quit. He works furiously, trying to use up the rest of the bricks and the mortar, and his enthusiasm infects his comrades. Finally, Tyurin has to order Ivan's trowel to be taken away from him, but Ivan continues to work with his own trowel, one which he had stashed away secretly.

The rest of the prisoners are ready to be counted for the return march, but Ivan will still not quit. Finally, after taking one last satisfied look at his work, he hides his trowel and runs to the roll call.

This episode is the climax of the story. Ivan's furious absorption in his work makes him *virtually a free man* for a few hours. He is reluctant to let go of this sense of freedom and individuality, and his enthusiasm is shared by some of his fellow prisoners for awhile. But they do not feel Ivan's deep, unique sense of personal fulfillment. When it is time to quit, they are pulled back into the grim reality of prison life much sooner than Ivan, who wants to finish his work properly, "even if the guards would set their dogs on him." Ivan's work reaffirms his worth as a human being in spite of the inhuman conditions under which he has to live. As he lovingly takes a last look at the straight lines of "his" wall, he is reassured that "his hands were still good for something."

Ivan Speculates about Faith and Astronomy

Ivan and Klevshin are greeted by derision and curses from the men whom they have kept waiting in the cold. As the ritual of the counting of the prisoners begins, Ivan reveals in a conversation with the Captain that he is indeed a simple, superstitious Russian peasant: he believes that the moon which they see rising is a new one every month and that the old one is broken up into stars by God. New stars, according to Ivan, are constantly needed because the old ones fall from the sky. Yet, in spite of these rather pagan opinions, Ivan asserts that he believes in God.

The head count reveals that a man is missing; it turns out to be a prisoner from another gang who has fallen asleep in the repair shop, and the five hundred men whom he has kept waiting for half an hour hurl abuses at him and even assault him physically, because he has deprived them of precious minutes of comparative leisure back in camp. Finally, the column begins its long march home.

Here in this episode, the reality of preparing to go back to camp is an anticlimax to Ivan's frenzied happiness while he was at work. Slowly, reality begins to overtake him, and the battle for survival which had been suspended for a few hours must be fought again.

Ivan's simple-minded statements concerning the lunar orbit reveal his naive faith in a pantheistic God, and he is looked at with disbelief by the educated Captain. To Ivan, God is revealed in nature. Note in particular that the Captain's sneering about Ivan's ignorance does not disturb Ivan at all. As in his later discussion with Alyosha, Ivan reveals an instinctive faith which needs no sophisticated theological argument. He is full of old Russian peasant superstitions, and Solzhenitsyn considers such faith to be superior to an adherence to the superficial rules of the Russian Orthodox church or to Alyosha's impractical Baptist beliefs.

Solzhenitsyn's distrust of intellectuals is once again shown. Here, in the discussion between the Captain and Caesar Markovich about *Potemkin,* another film by Sergei Eisenstein, Ivan overhears the part of the discussion which deals with a graphic visual scene in the film, in which the sailors on the battleship *Potemkin* are fed rotten meat, crawling with maggots. While the two connoisseurs discuss the artistic merit of this scene and other scenes in the film, they conclude, as an afterthought, that the prisoners in their own camp would eat such meat if it were served to them, presumably without revolting, as the sailors on the *Potemkin* eventually did. The reality of prison camp life, however, is far harsher than the "artistic imagery" of a film or a book; this may be a comment by Solzhenitsyn about the fact that even a starkly realistic work like *One Day in the Life of Ivan Denisovich* is incapable of adequately describing the grim reality of an isolated, freezing cold Siberian prison camp.

An Unexpected Race Homeward

Now that the men know that they will be the last ones back in camp and the last ones to eat the evening meal, their march homeward is slow and melancholy. Ivan remembers that he had been trying to get on the sicklist that very morning; he decides that it is a waste of time to try again.

Suddenly, another column of prisoners comes into view, and the remainder of the trip home turns into a race, trying to beat the other prisoners back to camp, since they know that the other gang comes from the tool works and are given an especially thorough frisking. They manage to win the race, and Ivan offers to go to the package room to look for a parcel that might have come for Caesar Markovich. Of course, he hopes to be rewarded for his troubles.

In this episode, note that the prisoners march slowly in order to get even with the guards for keeping them waiting for so long; they are exercising this tiny bit of power by "getting even." When they sight the other column of prisoners, however, their competitive spirit is aroused, and their once-slow march turns into a race, a change of mind which no official command could have achieved.

During this episode, we find out why the Captain is in the "special" camp. He had been detached, at one time, as a liaison officer to the allied British navy during World War II, and the British admiral to whom he had been assigned sent him a little gift after the war, with the inscription "In gratitude." The result of this innocent little gift was a twenty-five-year sentence for "rendering assistance to the enemy" – in spite of the fact that Great Britain was Russia's ally during the war.

Toward the end of the march, Ivan deplores the lack of solidarity among the prisoners; he states that the worst enemy of a prisoner is "the guy next to him. If they did not fight each other, it'd be another story." It seems that Solzhenitsyn's statement here is meant to apply not only to Ivan's prison camp, but to Russia as a whole. In his opinion, the Stalinist regime can stay in power only because the Russian population is divided against one another. If this were not so, the author indicates, Russia's fate might be vastly different.

The Risky Search

Just before he is to be searched prior to his entry back into camp, Ivan discovers the piece of steel in one of his pockets, the piece of steel that he picked up at the worksite in the morning. If the guards find it on him, it will mean ten days in solitary confinement. He is undecided whether or not to throw the incriminating potential weapon into the snow or to try and smuggle it through the search and, later, turn it into a small, valuable tool. His practical sense conquers his fear, and he hides the piece of steel in one of his mittens. He is lucky enough to have the guard miss it when he is frisked.

This is the third time that Ivan has exposed himself to the potential anger of the authorities. First, he was lucky not to be punished more severely for sleeping in late; then he took a chance in taking too long to finish his brick wall, and he made the guards wait for him. Now, he risks severe punishment by smuggling in a piece of steel, which could be defined as a weapon. Interestingly, this is the only time that we see Ivan pray to God. Later, he ungratefully expresses doubt in the efficacy of prayer. In any case, however, his prayer is answered, and he passes the inspection. The potential gain in his fight for survival – that is, he will be able to use the piece of steel to make extra money by using it as a knife or a tool – outweighs the risk of being caught.

At first, the importance of all three of these episodes might seem trivial: staying in bed a few moments too long, leaving work late, and accidentally pocketing a small piece of steel. These are hardly earth-shaking events in the world of the average reader, but, for Ivan, they are events which could be the difference between life and death. He is indeed lucky to escape all three incidents unscathed. The Moldavian, who fell asleep in the repair shop, and the Captain who voiced a rash but justified protest, were not so lucky. They may not survive the consequences of ten days in solitary confinement with reduced rations.

Markovich's Package

After his close call with the authorities, Ivan hurries to the package room to see if he can do Caesar Markovich a worthwhile favor by standing in line for him. As he waits, he remembers that in the Ust-Izhma camp, he received packages a couple of times. Since not much was left by the time the parcels reached him (many of the contents of these packages disappear when they are opened for "inspection"), Ivan has since instructed his wife not to send him any more parcels, particularly since he knows that his family back home has nothing to spare. Still, he sometimes hopes that a package will arrive for him unexpectedly. During his wait, he also finds out that the authorities will make the prisoners work on Sunday of next week, news which depresses Ivan, although he had expected it.

When Caesar finally arrives, he virtually disregards Ivan and begins a conversation about Moscow art events with another prison intellectual who is waiting for a package. They use a language which sounds foreign to Ivan, who has nothing but contempt for Moscow intellectuals. He suppresses his dislike for Caesar's intellectual snobbery and asks him if he can bring him his supper, but Caesar, as Ivan had hoped, lets him have his portion as a reward for waiting in line.

This part of the story contrasts Ivan, a have-not, with the wealthier prisoners who are lucky enough to receive additional food in packages from home. Even the supposedly egalitarian Soviet system has not eliminated "privilege," and the camp is a reflection of society as a whole. Ivan does not begrudge anybody the packages—some of the people he likes receive them. That is, Kilgas and Gopchik receive packages, but Ivan has decided that his own family cannot spare any food from home. Therefore, he has considerately forbidden his wife to send him any parcels. He knows that he can supplement his food rations by skill and cunning, and he enjoys his little rewards, like the extra bowl of mush at midday, more than if he were receiving food which he would know that his family could not spare.

Solzhenitsyn again shows his contempt for Caesar and his fellow intellectuals. In the scene in which Caesar ignores Ivan, who is doing him a favor, and engages in a lengthy discussion of the latest theater productions in Moscow, we see the black irony of the situation. That is, in the midst of starving men, such a discussion of "theater productions" (which none of the men will ever see) is absurd. But neither Caesar nor his fellow art connoisseur feel any affinity with the other prisoners and their fate. They themselves are well fed and can debate the latest issue of the *Moscow Evening News,* while Ivan has to struggle to survive. Soon afterward, Caesar has to rely on Ivan's cunning and loyalty – and on his hunger – to keep possession of the food in his package. In this scene, however, Caesar condescendingly lets Ivan have his supper – a morsel for a beggar.

Supper Rations

When Ivan returns to his barracks, there is a commotion because somebody's bread ration has been stolen while they were at work. Ivan finds his own bread intact in its hiding place and runs to the mess hall to join his gang for supper. In the mess hall, the manager and his orderlies are trying to keep order by using force when necessary. The fight for food is ruthless, and the otherwise meek Ivan brutally shoves a smaller prisoner out of the way when he needs a tray for his gang.

The food rations at supper are measured according to work output, and Ivan is rewarded for his good work by receiving a bigger bread portion than the others. In addition, he also has Caesar's portion, and so he contentedly settles down to his usual meal ritual. While he eats, he watches Y-81, a tall, old prisoner, and he thinks about what he has heard about the man, who has become a legend in the prison camps. After his meal, Ivan sets out to buy some tobacco from a Latvian in another barracks, a plan he put off in the morning on his way to the hospital.

In this episode, then, we see that after the elation of his bricklaying work and the joy of his luck at the search point, the depressing facts of camp life again fill Ivan's mind. Some bread (luckily, not his) has been stolen from his barracks, and the mess room orderlies,

prisoners themselves, tyrannize the inmates by exercising the miniscule amount of authority given to them by the authorities. Here,
Solzhenitsyn uses a theme which has been used in many works that
are set in prisons, prisoner-of-war camps, and in mental hospitals: that
is, the oppressed make the best oppressors. Other examples of this
can be found in Ken Kesey's *One Flew Over the Cuckoo's Nest,* in Henri
Charriere's *Papillon,* and in Tadeusz Borowski's concentration camp
novel, *This Way for the Gas, Ladies and Gentlemen.*

In this episode, Ivan is shown as less than perfect when he brutal-
izes a smaller and weaker prisoner in a fight for a food tray. In fact,
there are a number of small incidents in the story which show Ivan
in a less than saintly way, but this is the most negative one. Solzhenitsyn did not intend to make Ivan a "perfect" human being. Yet, in spite
of all his shortcomings, Ivan is still the model of the average Russian
"common man": kindhearted without being a saint, religious without
being a bigot, wise but not intellectual, cunning but not devious, practical and resourceful, yet not coldly calculating.

From the moment that he sits down to his "grand dinner" – two
bowls of thin gruel and a double bread portion – until the end of the
day, Ivan feels content. He even forgets about the extra work on
Sunday and about the two years which he still has to serve. But then
he comes face to face with his alter ego of the future: prisoner Y-81.

According to prison lore, Y-81 has been in prison longer than anybody else. Whenever one of his sentences has run out, another one
has been added on to it, and yet his back is still as straight as a ramrod.
He has lost all his hair and his teeth (Ivan has lost many of his own
teeth), and he takes no interest in anything or anybody around him.
He is determined never to give in, and he has developed his own rigid
code of behavior. His eating habits are impeccable; he does not put
his bread on the filthy table, but lays it on a clean rag. We are reminded that Ivan has begun to establish similar habits: he does not
eat loose fish eyes (only when they are still in the sockets); he has
never bribed anybody or taken a bribe. Solzhenitsyn insinuates that,
like Y-81, Ivan will not leave the prison camp, but he will not give
in. And he will survive because of his strength of will and his refusal
to compromise his human dignity.

Buying Tobacco

Ivan goes to Barracks 7 to buy some tobacco, thinking about the differences between the "special" camp and the previous camps he has known. In the "special" camp, prisoners do not get paid, while in Ust-Izhma, he was given at least thirty rubles a month. Here, Ivan makes extra money by doing odd jobs, such as making slippers for two rubles, or patching up jackets. He uses the money to buy tobacco at inflated prices from prisoners who get packages from home.

In the barracks of the Latvian from whom he buys his tobacco, Ivan listens to a conversation about the Korean War before he approaches his supplier. Then, he craftily haggles for as much tobacco as he can get into his shaving mug, the standard measure for such transactions. In between, he overhears other prisoners making derogatory comments about Stalin, and he contemplates the fact that the inmates of "special" camps are allowed much more freedom of expression than those in a "regular" camp, where such a remark would have been severely punished. There is, however, not much spare time to use this "freedom."

When Ivan gets back to his own barracks, he sees Caesar Markovich spread out the contents of his package on his bunk. Caesar has received some sausage, canned milk, a large smoked fish, sugar, butter, cigarettes, and some pipe tobacco—an unimaginable treasure for Ivan. Caesar generously lets Ivan keep his (Caesar's) supper bread ration, and Ivan is happy with this gift. He rationalizes to himself that packages create quite a bit of trouble for the people who receive them. They have to share their good fortune with many others—the guards, the gang boss, the barber, and the doctor. Ivan considers all this a mixed blessing. He is happy that he does not rely on other people. He does not envy Caesar, as many of the other prisoners do.

Here, the tobacco episode shows Ivan, once again, to be a crafty, practical man; he is clever enough to avoid being taken advantage of in any transaction. While he was paid rubles in the other camps, he was not able to use the money the way he would have liked to. Here, he has to do extra work to make a few rubles, but he can buy much better tobacco on the camp's "black market." As usual, Ivan is able to see the positive side of his situation and does not dwell on the disadvantages, another strong weapon in his survival arsenal.

Without comment, Solzhenitsyn introduces another conversation into this episode, this time about the Korean War and the possibility of its widening into a worldwide war after the Chinese intervention. Ivan, who has come for a practical purpose—to buy tobacco—is not at all interested in this topic. It is as irrelevant to his personal struggle for survival as a debate about Eisenstein films or the latest Moscow theatrical productions. The Korean War or, for that matter, a world war, will not change Ivan's situation substantially. Talking about it is a waste of precious spare time.

The comment by a prisoner about "that old bastard in Moscow with the mustache [who] wouldn't give a damn about his own brother" is the author's only direct reference to Stalin in the whole work. It is claimed that Khrushchev, through the editor of the first edition of *One Day in the Life of Ivan Denisovich*, wanted at least one direct, negative comment made about Stalin, whose policies he was trying to undo. This passage was Solzhenitsyn's way of complying with this request. Significantly, he chooses to refer to Stalin as "that old bastard in Moscow with the mustache," almost literally the same expression which he himself used in his correspondence with a friend; earlier, his correspondence and this reference were the reasons for Solzhenitsyn's imprisonment. Here in camp, however, the authorities don't even bother to punish such irreverence – a meaningless leniency which Ivan naively interprets as "freedom of speech." We must remember, however, that the Captain will spend ten hard days in solitary confinement for a more innocent and a more justified remark. In addition, there is not much time in this "special" camp to engage in "free speech," and Ivan considers any abstract discussion a waste of time.

Back in his barracks again, Ivan demonstrates that he is a reasonable, practical man. He looks at the assortment of Caesar's riches without envy and even realizes that such packages are a mixed blessing. He himself is able to provide the small luxuries he needs for himself by craftiness and hard work, and thus, he does not have to bribe anybody or defend and share his "wealth." In addition, he has seen ample evidence that packages do not come regularly enough to be relied on. He has observed many of these privileged people scrounging when their parcels did not show up. Ivan is content with Caesar's extra bread ration, and the extra food he has been able to get on this day, as well as some tobacco. His self-reliance will guarantee his chance for survival. But what will Caesar and the others do if their packages from home do not arrive?

Ivan Reviews the Day

Ivan settles down for a few small moments of relaxation before the evening roll call and lights-out. He considers several ways that he can use the little piece of steel which he has smuggled in. Then he hides it in a safe place.

Fetyukov come- into the barracks crying. He has been beaten up by somebody, probably for scrounging, and although he dislikes the man, Ivan feels sorry for him because he is certain that Fetyukov will not survive the camps.

Caesar Markovich still has the contents of his package spread out on his bunk when he asks Ivan for his little illegal knife so that he can cut some meat. He doesn't share his food with Ivan, though; he shares his food with the Captain, the only man in the gang whom he considers his equal. This meal, however, is only a short reprieve for Buynovsky, who is led away shortly afterward to the punishment block.

When the signal for the evening roll call is given, Caesar does not know what to do with his package. It is certain that most of it will be stolen by a prisoner or a guard while he is outside in the line-up. In spite of the fact that Caesar has treated him condescendingly all through the day, Ivan feels sorry for him and shows him a way to protect his food.

After the tedious daily routine of the roll call, Ivan and the other prisoners return to their bunks, find a place to dry their boots, and settle down for the night. Ivan, however, does not feel like sleeping; he is too elated about the many good things which have happened to him during the day. He is grateful that he has not ended up in a cell like the Captain and that he can even enjoy sleeping on his sheetless, sawdust mattress.

Ivan's day, then, is coming to a close on an upbeat note. He has successfully braved all the difficulties of the work day. More than that, he has been able to acquire some small luxuries which will help him during future days. The little piece of steel will allow him to make additional money, he has bread left over for the next day, and he has enough tobacco for awhile. Best of all, he has acquired all these benefits without having to compromise his dignity. In this generous mood, he even feels sorry for the scavenger Fetyukov, whom he sees humiliated and crying.

Ivan's generosity and basic good nature is further shown by his offer to assist Caesar Markovich, who considers himself so much better than the simple peasant Ivan. It is that same "simple peasant"

Ivan, however, who must come to his aid when the contents of Caesar's food package are threatened; knowledge of "art" and an upper-class background are of no practical use within the grim reality of the prison camp. Caesar's preoccupation with art may provide a temporary escape from prison life, but only Ivan's pragmatism and level-headedness can guarantee survival.

How close they all are to annihilation is demonstrated by the Captain's being led away to the prison block. And even at the last moment, he reveals that he is not as well prepared to survive as Ivan. If he could have stalled a little longer, he might have had at least a temporary reprieve. Instead, he responds immediately to his name being called.

The rest of the prisoners, while feeling sorry for him, are unable to provide him with more than trite encouragement – because, here, but for the grace of God, they all go.

The battle for survival even extends to the drying of the boots; it is every man for himself when they try to find a place close to the stove for their footwear; the unlucky ones will have to brave a day in damp boots and the danger of frostbite. It is bitter irony to hear Ivan thank God for his having had such a "good day" as he prepares for sleep, still giddy with joy over his several "successes" during the day.

Small but Important Triumphs

Alyosha the Baptist hears Ivan's mumbled "Thank God" and asks him why he does not pray more often. Ivan answers that he does not believe in the efficacy of prayer. His pragmatic nature does not place much stock in matters of the spirit, and his personal acquaintance with a worldly and corrupt priest of the Russian Orthodox church in his home village have made him cynical about organized religion. He again affirms his belief in God, but he expresses his skepticism about the outer trappings of religion and its complicated, dogmatic points. Religion does not provide him with a satisfactory explanation for his fate. Consequently, he has no use for it.

When the prisoners are called out for a second roll call, Caesar Markovich shows that he has learned his lesson. He gives Ivan cookies, sugar, and some sausage for his help in protecting his package. When they return, Ivan voluntarily shares some of it with Alyosha and thinks about what he will do with the rest. As he falls asleep, he recounts the triumphs of this day:

(1) he has not been put into solitary confinement;
(2) his gang has not been reassigned to a new, harder worksite;
(3) he has managed to get an extra bowl of mush at lunch;
(4) Tyurin has gotten them good work rates;
(5) he has smuggled a valuable piece of metal into camp;
(6) he was given extra food by Caesar in the evening; and
(7) he was able to buy some tobacco.

This has indeed been an extraordinarily happy day, and as Ivan drifts off into sleep, he recalls that there are 3,653 days in his sentence; the extra three are due to leap years.

A contented Ivan explains why he rejects organized religion. He compares prayers to the complaints which the prisoners are allowed to put into boxes set up for this purpose in the camp. Either there is no answer, or they come back marked "Rejected." Alyosha tries to persuade Ivan with dogma, but the pragmatic Ivan is unprepared to accept the symbolism of mountains moved by prayer. His literal mind equates the "daily bread" of the Lord's Prayer to the prison rations, and he cannot imagine God moving any mountains in spite of Alyosha's intensive prayers.

When he confronts Alyosha with the cruel facts of worldly, corrupt priests, the young man winces. There is very little he can respond with, except to say that the Baptist church is less corrupt than the Russian Orthodox church. Alyosha's final argument – that his imprisonment is cause for rejoicing because it gives him a chance to contemplate and strengthen his faith – is met with a resigned silence by Ivan. What he wants is an explanation for his being imprisoned. Alyosha can take solace in the fact that he is a martyr for his faith, but Ivan is here, in the prison camp, because Russia was not prepared for World War II in 1941. She sent him to the front lines ill-equipped, to be taken prisoner by superior German forces, and then punished him for that. For Ivan, religion provides no satisfactory answers for such anguished questions as "Why am I here?" and "Was it my fault?"

At some point, Ivan even expresses doubt that he still wants to regain his freedom. First of all, he does not know whether he will really be released at the end of his term. Second, he doubts that he will be allowed to go home and rejoin his family, even if he is released.

52

Third, and most depressing, he does not know any longer *where* he would be better off.

It is easy to understand that a prisoner, after eight years, would have many doubts concerning whether or not he would be able to readjust to life outside the camp. The stable prison routine, despite all its cruelty, could begin to seem like a safe, comfortable place.

Ivan's Code of Survival

The final paragraphs of this short novel are the most memorable ones. After our initial horror at the inhumane conditions of life in a "special" camp, the reader gradually begins to see Ivan's day through the eyes of a man who has become used to much of this horror and, unlike the reader, is no longer angry, or even dejected, about his condition. Such emotions would be a waste of time and would detract from his efforts to survive and, if possible, to improve his lot. Thus, Ivan takes most of the outrages of camp life for granted; he spends his energy trying to cope with unexpected dangers. Finally, even the reader adopts Ivan's stance. If one accepts the everyday camp conditions as natural and unalterable, as Ivan does, then the protagonist has indeed had an "almost happy" day.

CRITICAL ESSAYS

LEVELS OF MEANING IN THE NOVEL

• **A Prison Novel.** Most worthwhile pieces of literature operate on multiple levels of meaning. One of these is the literal level – that is, a level on which one requires only an understanding of the basic denotation of the terms and concepts employed by the author. Expressed simply, on this level the author communicates with the reader in a "realistic," non-symbolic fashion. The reader has to transfer very few terms and concepts to a non-literal, symbolic or allegorical level.

One Day in the Life of Ivan Denisovich is literally a prison story, and thus, it takes its place in a long list of similar works which deal with conditions in prisons, labor camps, concentration camps, mental hospitals, or POW camps. As such, it deals with many of the same problems that works like *The Survivor* by Terrence des Pres, Pierre Boulle's *The Bridge on the River Kwai,* Borowski's *This Way for the Gas,*

Ladies and Gentlemen, Henri Charriere's *Papillon,* and many German, French, and British POW novels attempt to come to grips with.

Like all of these works, *One Day in the Life of Ivan Denisovich* deals with the struggle for survival under inhumane conditions. What must a man or a woman do to get out of such a camp alive? Is survival the only and most important goal, or are there limits to what a person can and should do to stay alive? Is religious faith necessary or vital for survival? All of these are questions which this work attempts to answer on a literal level.

Solzhenitsyn, who has first-hand experience of the camp conditions which he describes in this story, relates the actual experiences of millions of his compatriots, and his Russian readers could not help but ponder the real possibility of their being confronted with Ivan Denisovich's situation.

Like the authors of other prison novels, Solzhenitsyn concludes that it is the duty of a human being not to resign and give up the struggle for survival. However, it is wrong to concentrate on what one must do to survive. It is better to establish a personal code of behavior which dictates *what one will not do* just to preserve one's physical existence.

Existence without dignity is worthless—in fact, loss of human dignity will also diminish the will and the capacity to survive. Compromises are certainly necessary, but there is a vast moral gap between Ivan and Fetyukov: Fetyukov will do anything for a little more food, and he is properly referred to as a scavenging animal; Ivan, in contrast, will swindle and bully, at times, but basically, he relies on his resourcefulness to achieve the same goal. He does not lick bowls, he does not give or take bribes, and he is deferential when necessary, but he never crawls. With some improvement in his habits of personal hygiene, he will probably, eventually, become what might be termed "the ideal prisoner," represented by Y-81, the meticulous old camp inmate whom Ivan admires.

Survival is a task which needs Ivan's constant, simple-minded attention. Abstractions, esoteric discussions on religion or on art are irrelevant and counter-productive. Caesar Markovich can survive only as long as his packages arrive. The Captain, if he survives solitary confinement, will have to give up his unrealistic ideas about communism and his overbearing manner if he wants to live. Alyosha the Baptist is, by the very nature of his faith, more interested in an afterlife than he is in physical survival during this lifetime. Clearly, Fetyukov and most of the informers will not live long.

Only Ivan combines all the qualities necessary to survive: he works for himself and for his comrades, but not for the authorities; he does not rely on outside help, but on his own skill and craftiness; he is used to obeying sensible orders and circumventing absurd ones; he has faith, but it is a faith designed to help him cope with the realities of this life, not one which exhausts itself in dogmatic theological debate. Ivan believes in the strength and the dignity of the simple Russian worker and peasant without being a doctrinaire Communist. He is, with some lapses, a compassionate human being who looks at his fellow prisoners with sympathy and understanding. Most of them appreciate this attitude and treat him with the same respect.

• **A Social Commentary.** The population of Ivan's prison camp contains a cross section of Russian society. There are prisoners representing virtually every professional, social, and ethnic group in the Soviet Union: we find artists, intellectuals, criminals, peasants, former government officials, officers, Ukrainians, Latvians, Estonians, and gypsies (Caesar Markovich), just to name a few. If one looks, therefore, beyond the literal level of the novel, it becomes clear that Solzhenitsyn not only wanted to give a realistic description of life in a Siberian prison camp, but that he also wanted the reader to understand that the camp—on an allegorical level—was a representation of Stalinist Soviet Russia.

In an interview, Solzhenitsyn once stated that he had been interested in a statement made by Leo Tolstoy, who said that a novel could deal with either centuries of European history, or with one day in a man's life. (This statement by Tolstoy may have also been the reason why Solzhenitsyn changed the title of this work from *S-854* to *One Day in the Life of Ivan Denisovich*.) During his own prison term, the author made up his mind to describe one day of prison life, one day in the life of Ivan Denisovich Shukhov, whose fate Solzhenitsyn once called "the greatest tragedy in Russian drama."

Read on this level, the novel becomes a scathing indictment of the Soviet system during the Stalin era. Solzhenitsyn would now certainly extend this indictment to the Soviet system as a whole. There are chronic food shortages, except for a privileged few who can bribe advantages out of corrupt officials. There is vandalism and bureaucratic inefficiency, leading to waste and sabotage. To dispel any doubt that all this applies only to camp life, Solzhenitsyn introduces Ivan's thoughts about the collective farm from which he comes ("Daydreams of Home and of the *Kolkhoz*"), which is barely functioning. The men there have bribed the officials to relieve them from farm work so they can paint the profitable, sleazy carpets. In addition, there is also the constant spying and informing activities which are typical of Soviet society, and Solzhenitsyn deplores them most of all, for they create distrust among people who should cooperate against the authorities rather than against themselves. A prisoner, he says, is another prisoner's worst enemy, not the authorities. It is interesting to note that, in spite of serving ten- or twenty-five-year sentences, all of the prisoners seem to be serving life terms. Nobody is ever released from the larger Soviet prison; when one term ends, another one is added on.

It was probably an accident that *One Day in the Life of Ivan Denisovich* was published exactly one hundred years after *Letters from the House of the Dead,* Dostoevsky's famous account of his own experiences in prison under the Czar. But certainly, many Russian readers would immediately recognize the connection between the two works and realize the irony inherent in the comparison: prisons under the hated Czars were, by far, more humane than those under Stalin, and far fewer people were imprisoned in them.

What can be done to overcome these wretched social conditions? It is clear that Solzhenitsyn sees as little possibility for a successful, violent overthrow of the Soviet regime as he does for an armed revolt in Ivan's camp. The real hope is that the corrupt, inefficient system will destroy itself from within, and that Russia will return to a system which is founded on the qualities which Ivan represents: hard work without too much reliance on technology.

Here, Solzhenitsyn follows Dostoevsky's anti-Western, anti-technological attitude. He calls for (1) a revival of the old Russian folk traditions, (2) a simple, mystic faith without the dogmatic bureaucracy of any established church, (3) cooperation between the multitudes of ethnic and social groups in Russia who are now divided and, thus, "their own worst enemies," and (4) an attitude of non-cooperation and non-violent undermining of the bureaucracy and the authorities.

Even if it appears that conditions will not change soon (another prison term may be added on), the actions of the Russian people should be designed to survive with dignity and pride, not with groveling and crawling. It should be noted that Solzhenitsyn does not expect any leadership from intellectuals, churchmen, or artists in this struggle. Their love for abstractions and endless discussion is shown as not producing practical results.

• **An Existential Commentary.** Beyond the literal and the social level, we can detect in this work a theme which aligns it closely to many works of modern fiction. Its theme is the fate of modern man who must make sense of a universe whose operations he does not understand. Thus, the level of meaning which addresses the questions "How is one to survive in a prison camp?" and "How is one to survive in the Soviet Union, which is like a prison camp?" is extended to this question: "According to what principles should one live in a seemingly absurd universe, controlled by forces which one can't understand and over which one has no control?"

Ivan's fate closely resembles that of Josef K. in Franz Kafka's *The Trial*. Josef K. is arrested one morning without knowing why, and he attempts to find out the reasons. In his search, he encounters a cruel court bureaucracy which operates according to incomprehensible rules; lawyers and priests cannot provide him with reasonable answers for his fate, and so he finally concludes that he must be guilty. Accordingly, he willingly submits to his execution.

Ivan is also arrested and sent to prison camps for absurd reasons, and so are most of his fellow inmates. He does not understand the legalities of his case. He is, after all, only a simple worker, and he never encounters the highest authorities who might provide him with an answer. He meets only cruel, minor officials of the system, who only obey orders but do not give explanations. The intellectuals around him do not seem to have the right answers, and the religious people, like Alyosha the Baptist, are very similar to the comforters who try to explain to Job the reason why he must suffer so cruelly. Their arguments are dogmatic; they are not logical or practical.

A man who finds himself in such a situation has several options. One is despair, a passive acceptance of whatever fate has in store for him. This, as Camus indicates in *The Myth of Sisyphus*, is unacceptable behavior for an intelligent human being. An extension of that option is suicide, an alternative that is not even mentioned in *One Day in the Life of Ivan Denisovich*.

Another alternative is to search for a system of thought which will provide an explanation for such a basic existential question as "Why is all this happening to me?" These could be philosophical, religious, or political systems of thought, most of them having spokesmen who seemingly are able to give answers. Unfortunately, they all require that a person accepts at least one basic point of dogma *on faith* — that is, one must not ask for proof. And that is unacceptable to many practical, logical people like Ivan. Therefore, Ivan must ultimately reject Alyosha the Baptist's interpretation of the universe.

Despite the fact that Ivan does believe in God, albeit a pantheistic pagan god, his answer to the existential question of modern man is fundamentally that of Jean-Paul Sartre and other Existentialists. He decides to adopt a personal code of behavior similar to that of Hemingway's so-called "code heroes," whose highest satisfaction is derived from demonstrating "grace under pressure." Rather than adopting other people's behavioral codes (for example, the Ten Commandments), Ivan establishes his own set of morals, which are designed to help him survive with dignity. Since nobody can give him a logical explanation for his fate, he abandons all attempts at finding such an explanation and structures his life by the premise that there is, in fact, none. This allows him to concentrate on gaining satisfaction from following the standards he has set for himself. He does not have to please anyone about practical matters. This is graphically demonstrated by Ivan, particularly in his sense of self-reliance and in his "grace under pressure" behavior. He is a prototype of what Sartre calls a man "living in good faith," as well as a prototype for the common Russian, in whom Solzhenitsyn puts his hope for a better future.

STYLE AND NARRATIVE PERSPECTIVE

The choice of a protagonist created a problem of narration for Solzhenitsyn. Ivan is certainly not *un*intelligent, but his educational background is not suited for narrating a lengthy story. On the other hand, it would not have been suitable to have a highly educated narrator tell us about Ivan, because the educational and emotional distance between the two would have been too great. First-person narration by Ivan and third-person omniscient narration were therefore not possible. Solzhenitsyn uses a form of narration in *One Day in the Life of Ivan Denisovich* which is an ingenious variation of a traditional Russian narrative form, the *skaz*. This technique, employed widely in Russian folk tales, establishes an anonymous narrator who is on the same educational and social level as the protagonist and is able to transmit the main character's actions and thoughts, using the third-person singular, and sometimes the first-person plural, but giving the impression to the reader that the story is being told in first person by the protagonist. Indeed, in *One Day*, the reader has the impression that Ivan is the narrator, and only a closer look reveals that most of the story is told in third person. The reader sees through Ivan's eyes, although Ivan is *not* the narrator.

In addition to the *skaz* narrator, Solzhenitsyn employs another narrator who could be an educated fellow prisoner – the persona of the author – who is used only when the story has to deal with concepts which are clearly beyond the intellectual and linguistic grasp of both Ivan and the anonymous *skaz* narrator.

In yet other instances, this anonymous alter ego of Ivan's is present, but unable to penetrate into Ivan's mind. In these cases, we are told Ivan's thoughts in the third person, but in Ivan's own words; this perspective is mainly used for Ivan's daydreams.

We can thus discern three different narrative perspectives in *One Day in the Life of Ivan Denisovich*:

1. a prisoner (*skaz*) narrator who is on Ivan's intellectual level, but who has a greater gift for narration; he uses mainly third person, but will fall into first-person plural (we, us) when he wants to stress communality between Ivan, the other prisoners, and himself.

2. an omniscient, educated narrator, who is more or less the mouthpiece for the author's philosophical views.

3. Ivan himself, though using third person, mainly describing flashbacks and daydreams.

Once the reader is aware of these differences in point-of-view, it becomes easy to differentiate between the narrators.

> "Some fellows always thought the grass was greener on the other side of the fence. Let them envy other people if they wanted to, but Ivan knew what life was about."

This is clearly the *skaz* narrator speaking, characterized by the informal language and the choice of words.

> "With the same swift movements, Shukhov hung his overcoat on a crossbeam, and from under the mattress he pulled out his mittens, a pair of thin foot-cloths, a bit of rope, and a piece of rag with two tapes."

This is obviously the educated, omniscient third-person narrator.

> "What was the point of telling them what gang you
> worked in and what your boss was like? Now you had
> more in common with that Latvian Kilgas than with your
> own family."

This is Ivan marching along to the worksite in the morning, thinking about the letter which he will probably *not* write to his wife.

The most important function of this separation of points-of-view and the reason why Solzhenitsyn did not want to present the events in first person, through Ivan's eyes, is his intention of giving an "objective" picture of this day in Ivan's life, a goal that would have been diminished by the use of the highly subjective first-person point-of-view. Had Ivan told his own story, the reader might dismiss much of what is stated as opinion, lack of insight, or outright bias. Solzhenitsyn's method allows us to see Ivan objectively from the outside through the eyes of two anonymous fellow prisoners—one educated, the other on Ivan's peasant level—but still sharing the inner thoughts and feelings of the protagonist.

QUESTIONS FOR REVIEW

1. What is the significance of the scenes in which Caesar Markovich discusses films by Sergei Eisenstein with other intellectuals?

2. Consider the fact that the reader is never given a view of the Camp Commandant. What may be the reasons for the absence of this stock figure of prison novels?

3. What is Solzhenitsyn trying to say when he states that "the prisoner's worst enemy is the guy next to him"?

4. What is the purpose of having so many different factions of Russian society represented in the camp?

5. What is the relationship between Ivan Denisovich Shukhov and prisoner Y-81?

6. Why does Ivan forbid his wife to send him packages with food? Is there another, more important reason than the one given by Ivan himself?

7. Why is Captain Buynovsky in this "special" camp? Is his reason for having been jailed substantially different from the other prisoners?

8. What is the deeper meaning of the fact that most prisoners have new sentences added on when their original ones expire?

9. Why are escape attempts from the camp not only hopeless but also absurd?

10. What is Ivan's (Solzhenitsyn's) attitude toward intellectuals and artists? Do you think it is justified? Only in Russia, or elsewhere as well?

SUGGESTED THEME TOPICS

1. *One Day in the Life of Ivan Denisovich* can be read on three different levels of meaning. Give a coherent review of each, providing examples from the work and show how the three levels are related to each other.

2. *Cancer Ward* is another work by Alexander Solzhenitsyn which deals with life in a Soviet prison. Show the similarities and dissimilarities in the two works.

3. Leo Tolstoy has said that a novel can deal with either centuries of European history or with one day in one man's life. Show how this short novel deals with both one day in Ivan Denisovich Shukhov's life and with a piece of European history at the same time.

4. Compare *One Day in the Life of Ivan Denisovich* with one or more prison or POW novels (some titles have been suggested in this text).

5. Give a brief, interpretive comparison between the award-winning play and motion picture *Stalag 17* and *One Day in the Life of Ivan Denisovich.* Is it possible to imagine a humorous treatment of Solzhenitsyn's theme?

SELECTED BIBLIOGRAPHY

BAUER, DANIEL J. "An Existential Look at Solzhenitsyn's Ivan Denisovich." *Fu Jen Studies: Literature & Linguistics.* Taipei, Taiwan, Republic of China 12:17–38, 1979.

CISMARU, ALFRED. "The Importance of Food in *One Day in the Life of Ivan Denisovich*," in *San Jose Studies* 9/1 (1983), pp. 99–105.

ERICSON, EDWARD E. *Solzhenitsyn: The Moral Vision.* Grand Rapids, 1980.

FEUER, KATHRYN, ed. *Solzhenitsyn: A Collection of Critical Essays.* Englewood Cliffs, 1976.

KODJAK, ANDREJ. *Alexander Solzhenitsyn.* Boston, 1978.

LUPLOW, RICHARD. "Narrative Style and Structure in *One Day in the Life of Ivan Denisovich*." *Russian Literature Triquarterly,* Ann Arbor, Michigan, 1(1971): 399–412.

MATTHEWS, IRENE J. "A. Solzhenitsyn's *One Day in the Life of Ivan Denisovich*," in *The Humanities Association Review.* 23/ii (1972), pp. 8–13.

MOODY, CHRISTOPHER. *Solzhenitsyn.* New York, 1976.

RUTTNER, ECKHARD. "The Names in Solzhenitsyn's Short Novel, *One Day in the Life of Ivan Denisovich*," in *Journal of the American Name Society.* 23(1975), pp. 103–11.

SCAMMELL, MICHAEL. *Solzhenitsyn: A Biography.* New York, 1981.

NOTES

Your Guides to Successful Test Preparation.

Cliffs Test Preparation Guides
• *Complete* • *Concise* • *Functional* • *In-depth*

Efficient preparation means better test scores. Go with the experts and use *Cliffs Test Preparation Guides*. They focus on helping you know what to expect from each test, and their test-taking techniques have been proven in classroom programs nationwide. Recommended for individual use or as a part of a formal test preparation program.

Publisher's ISBN Prefix 0-8220

Qty.	ISBN	Title	Price	Qty.	ISBN	Title	Price
	2078-5	ACT	8.95		2044-0	Police Sergeant Exam	9.95
	2069-6	CBEST	8.95		2047-5	Police Officer Exam	14.95
	2056-4	CLAST	9.95		2049-1	Police Management Exam	17.95
	2071-8	ELM Review	8.95		2076-9	Praxis I: PPST	9.95
	2077-7	GED	11.95		2017-3	Praxis II: NTE Core Battery	14.95
	2061-0	GMAT	9.95		2074-2	SAT*	9.95
	2073-4	GRE	9.95		2325-3	SAT II*	14.95
	2066-1	LSAT	9.95		2072-6	TASP	8.95
	2046-7	MAT	12.95		2079-3	TOEFL w/cassettes	29.95
	2033-5	Math Review	8.95		2080-7	TOEFL Adv. Prac. (w/cass.)	24.95
	2048-3	MSAT	24.95		2034-3	Verbal Review	7.95
	2020-3	Memory Power for Exams	5.95		2043-2	Writing Proficiency Exam	8.95

Prices subject to change without notice.

Available at your booksellers, or send this form with your check or money order to **Cliffs Notes, Inc., P.O. Box 80728, Lincoln, NE 68501** http://www.cliffs.com

☐ Money order   ☐ Check payable to Cliffs Notes, Inc.

☐ Visa ☐ Mastercard   Signature_____

Card no. _____ Exp. date _____

Signature _____

Name _____

Address _____

City _____State_____ Zip_____

*GRE, MSAT, Praxis PPST, NTE, TOEFL and Adv. Practice are registered trademarks of ETS.
SAT is a registered trademark of CEEB.

Think Quick

Now there are more Cliffs Quick Review® titles, providing help with more introductory level courses. Use Quick Reviews to increase your understanding of fundamental principles in a given subject, as well as to prepare for quizzes, midterms and finals.

Do better in the classroom, and on papers and tests with Cliffs Quick Reviews.

Publisher's ISBN Prefix 0-8220

Qty.	ISBN	Title	Price	Total	Qty.	ISBN	Title	Price	Total
	5309-8	Accounting Principles I	9.95			5330-6	Human Nutrition	9.95	
	5302-0	Algebra I	7.95			5331-4	Linear Algebra	9.95	
	5303-9	Algebra II	9.95			5333-0	Microbiology	9.95	
	5300-4	American Government	9.95			5326-8	Organic Chemistry I	9.95	
	5301-2	Anatomy & Physiology	9.95			5335-7	Physical Geology	9.95	
	5304-7	Basic Math & Pre-Algebra	7.95			5337-3	Physics	7.95	
	5306-3	Biology	7.95			5327-6	Psychology	7.95	
	5312-8	Calculus	7.95			5349-7	Statistics	7.95	
	5318-7	Chemistry	7.95			5358-6	Trigonometry	7.95	
	5320-9	Differential Equations	9.95			5360-8	United States History I	7.95	
	5324-1	Economics	7.95			5361-6	United States History II	7.95	
	5329-2	Geometry	7.95			5367-5	Writing Grammar, Usage, & Style	9.95	

Prices subject to change without notice.

Available at your booksellers, or send this form with your check or money order to **Cliffs Notes, Inc., P.O. Box 80728, Lincoln, NE 68501** http://www.cliffs.com

☐ Money order ☐ Check payable to Cliffs Notes, Inc.

☐ Visa ☐ Mastercard   Signature_____

Card no. _____ Exp. date_____

Name _____

Address _____

City _____State_____ Zip_____

Telephone (_____)_____